Kingston Court

A Novel

HOLLY KAMMIER

Cover design by Ebook Launch
Author photo by Patrick Griffin

Book formatted by Louise Bohmer:
http://www.louisebohmer.com/site/freelance/

ISBN-13: 978-0-9963788-9-5

DEDICATION

*This is dedicated to all my beautiful, feisty girlfriends.
I wrote this book for you.*

You've always had the power my dear, you just had to learn it for yourself.
– Glinda, The Wizard of Oz

NATALIE: MAY 22, 2014

I loved the Gaslamp Quarter at night. Here I got to wear heels instead of New Balance, trade my sweats for a little black dress and red lips. The city made me sexy.

It was a tranquil Thursday in late spring and I should have been hanging out with my mommy friends on Kingston Court. Once a week, without fail, we met up in the cul-de-sac with our kiddos in the evening to drink wine and catch up on all the neighborhood gossip. Tonight was special though. I had a date with my favorite man.

My husband Mark shifted the gears of our BMW as I peered up at the passing lights and giant fashion ads painted on the brick walls of San Diego's classic building facades. Victorian era architecture mixed with modern skyscrapers. The din of traffic and dingy smell of the streets made me forget to worry over ladies' night or our two children at home. At least for this moment, we were young again.

Mark slid a hand against my bare thigh as we slowed at a light. "Wanna ditch dinner and find a dark alley?"

The subtle streaks of his greying hair were hidden in the dimly lit sports sedan, turning him into a darker, more mysterious, version of himself. I laughed and leaned toward him, kissing the freckle below his ear. "Tempting. Very tempting. If I wasn't so hungry I might take you up on that."

I breathed in his citrus scented after-shave, as I wrapped my hand around his bicep. Mark flexed his arm and narrowed his green eyes at me. "You sure?" he teased in a low voice, almost like a growl. "I get all crazy when you dress like that."

"Shoot." My eyebrows sank as I glanced down at my open purse. A small green toothbrush sat on top of my wallet.

"What?"

"I have Ben's toothbrush."

My husband and I looked at each other in resignation.

"Jamie is watching him. Maybe it'll be fine," I said, though we both knew it wouldn't.

Our five-year-old son could be difficult. His most recent obsession was brushing his teeth after every meal. I could think of worse things for him to be insistent upon, but going to bed without his toothbrush of choice wasn't an option. It was only a matter of time before my best friend would call telling us to come home.

Mark's tired face turned stoic without the charm of his smile. He pulled into the next u-turn lane to head back for the freeway.

"Are you mad?" I asked, reaching for his knee.

"Eh, we'll just drop it off and swing by that Thai place you like." He shrugged and took my hand, reverting back to the role of comforting husband.

I scrunched up my nose and removed the barrette holding back my shoulder length brown hair. We were celebrating my thirty-eighth birthday and there was nothing romantic about the Taste of Thai at our neighborhood strip mall.

The light in front of us turned green, and I brushed my hand against the back of his neck, hoping to be absolved of my guilt. "Maybe we can still—"

He turned to look at me. His eyes, focused only on mine, carried none of the fear I suddenly felt wash over me. In that single moment life froze. I needed to speak, to take the wheel, something. Instead, I watched the set of headlights outside Mark's window get closer.

An intake of breath. A downpour of shattered glass. The sound of my scream as if it belonged to someone else.

The car lifted then tumbled. A dizzy Ferris wheel of lights …

NATALIE: THURSDAY, MAY 22

"Mrs. Delisse? I'm Jennifer from California General ER in La Jolla." I woke feeling battered and bruised, like I'd been in a bar fight and lost the battle. Bright fluorescent lights burned my eyes. I was lying in a sterile hospital bed, a wide-eyed young nurse looking over me in concern.

"Where's my husband?" Broken memories punched back at me. The scrape of my flesh against metal as hands pulled at me. There was the shriek of sirens and urgent questions. Now I was here. I needed to make sure Mark was okay.

The nurse, who had a small scar running from her upper lip to the bottom of her nose, tucked a strand of blonde hair behind her ear. I watched her right eyelid twitch in what appeared to be a nervous tick. "The two of you were in a car accident. You received a concussion, but your vital signs look good and you don't appear to have any significant injuries. Just some superficial cuts and bruises on your face and arms. We also put a few stitches on your right thigh."

"What about Mark?"

She flinched. "I'm afraid his injuries are serious." Her full sentences sounded like clipped words. "Head Trauma ... Possible brain damage ... Multiple fractures ... Very serious condition."

My stomach clenched. Senses heightened, I zeroed in on the tiny drops of crimson blood splattered across my starched white hospital sheets. "But he's going to be ok?"

"At this point we're not one hundred percent sure. The doctor inserted a chest tube for your husband's collapsed lung. We've taken multiple x-rays and sent him straight to surgery to stop the bleeding and mend his broken pelvis and femur. We should have another update for you soon."

My mind flashed to my injured husband lying helpless on a hospital gurney, bleeding, surrounded by bright lights and masked doctors. I imagined our children growing up without a father, me getting old alone. Why hadn't I said something when I saw those headlights coming at us? If I'd just opened my mouth and warned him.

"Mrs. Delisse, ma'am, are you feeling dizzy or lightheaded?" The young nurse's high-pitched voice yanked me back to my new reality.

"Why do I only have a few scratches and bruises? How could he have gotten so hurt if I'm fine?"

"He was in the line of impact. His head hit the roof when the car tumbled."

My mind went numb. "I need to see him. I need you to take me to him. Now."

SAMANTHA: THURSDAY, MAY 22

Cameron was cheating on me. I didn't have any proof yet, but I could sense it. He hadn't defended me when our oldest daughter attacked my parenting skills, nor had he made any attempts to seduce me in weeks. And that wasn't all.

He'd been wearing new underwear lately. I read somewhere that new underwear was a sure sign of infidelity. Then there was the extra time spent getting ready in the morning for class—more time shaving every wayward hair off his handsome face, brushing his thick brunette locks into a calculated, seemingly effortless style, picking out just the right pair of jeans and tailored, button down shirts that highlighted his tall, lean physique.

Cameron hadn't been this carefree and happy since

we planned our wedding.

I hated him.

I hated him for cheating on me. For making me feel less important than I already felt. Less needed, less attractive, less relevant in his life.

When we met, he couldn't get enough of me. He sought me out on the crowed dance floor of a popular San Francisco nightclub. He loved my laugh, my body, my clothes, the color of my butter-blonde hair in the morning light. Cameron introduced me to his friends and family, and put a gigantic sparkling ring on my finger. He talked about moving me into a beachside home somewhere in San Diego and fathering my children. He was everything I dreamed about. A kind, attractive, intelligent, man who wanted me and made it his mission to make me his wife.

That was twenty years ago. Now, digging through the dirty laundry basket in our bedroom I hadn't found a single shred of evidence. I had already torn through his drawers looking for any hidden panties or romantic gifts tucked away in the crevices. I had sniffed his shirts for the hint of a woman's scent. Nothing. There wasn't as much as a shoe out of place on his side of the closet either. Every polo shirt and every pair of slacks were hung and folded in just the right spot. He must have been hoarding whatever gifts, condoms, or love notes he intended for his mistress in his office at work.

The image of his lover invaded my mind. An eager, beautiful, younger version of me. Someone who seated herself in the front row of his upper-division history class at Cal State San Marcos, giggling at his jokes, lingering on every word he spoke, smiling in just the right places, and nodding during each pause. She would pay a visit to his small, private office after class with questions and to "discuss" his lectures. She would put her feet up on his desk to show off her long tanned legs, run slender fingers through her hair and lean in close to reveal the top of her flawless twenty-year-old tits.

I wanted to crush her, push her off a sheer cliff late at night when no one would be around to save her.

Tossing aside more dirty laundry, I found a fresh layer of limp undershirts and wrinkled boxer shorts. The first time I suspected Cameron of cheating was after he returned home from an extended faculty retreat. I had spent the entire week taking care of our three children on my own and was getting ready to do a load of delicates when I noticed his black slacks smelled funny, not like a woman, or food, but off somehow. They also had a weird whitish sheen on them, kind of like dried Elmer's glue. My heartbeat quickened and bile rose in my esophagus as I tossed them in the washer. That stain represented a direct threat.

These clothes didn't smell of perfume, lotion or anything else suspicious. There were no long loose hairs clinging to his discarded boxer shorts either.

Slumping to the floor, I didn't know whether to feel relieved or disappointed. A lack of evidence wasn't proof of his innocence.

NATALIE: SUNDAY, MAY 25

Three days after the accident, Mark's mother dragged her luggage off the carousel and searched for my face in the non-existent crowd. Waving like a child who didn't really want her name called, I caught her attention.

Elizabeth had grown older since her last visit. Just four months ago this robust, small-town beauty appeared ageless. Now her bright blue eyes resembled diluted pools of water, the lines in her face sunk deeper.

When we hugged, her stiff body collapsed into mine. Tears soaked my thin T-shirt. I hated to admit how good it felt to be with someone who hurt as much as I did, who felt this wound so deeply. Friends and extended family expressed shock and sadness, but Mark's accident didn't impact their daily lives. It didn't threaten to steal their only son away from them, or leave them with fatherless, children or a vegetable for a spouse.

"I can't believe this is happening." Elizabeth clung to me in my embrace. The weight of her long hair, dyed a hard black to remove any hint of gray, blanketed my arms.

"It doesn't feel real to me either. I keep thinking if we had celebrated my birthday a week earlier, or if I had just remembered to leave Ben's toothbrush at home. If I could go back in time and tell Mark to break or swerve or ..." My thoughts trailed off. Truth was, once we were in the crosshairs of that SUV, I don't know what I could have done to save us.

Elizabeth pulled away and looked at me, red rimming the pale blue of her eyes. "I've been doing the same thing, thinking of ways I could have changed the outcome somehow. Maybe if we hadn't let you talk Mark into staying here in San Diego. It could have completely changed everything. He's our only child." Her shoulders trembled.

My hands began to shake, wondering how badly Elizabeth wished it was me in the hospital instead of Mark. It didn't matter, I needed to hold it together. "Were you able to track down Tom before you left for the airport?"

"Yes, he knows everything." She stood a little straighter, sniffling and composing herself. "There's another strike going on in Paris and the airports are all shut down. It will take at least another day before he can fly out. Of all the times to be stuck outside the country on a business trip. He's beside himself that he can't be here for his son."

"Is there ever *not* a strike going on somewhere in France?" It felt nice to direct my frustration at something other than the details surrounding the accident, if only for a moment.

"Apparently not," Elizabeth agreed. "Where are the kids? Are they with your parents?"

"No, my mom and dad are still in Chicago, they'll be out tomorrow. The kids've been at the hospital with me. Jamie took them home a couple of hours ago."

"Are you sure that was the best idea? Seeing their daddy like that could damage them. Ben doesn't need any more problems than he already has."

I bit the side of my finger in anxiety. Elizabeth had been here a matter of minutes and she was already getting under my skin.

Trying to ignore the sting of her reprimand, I tugged at a piece of crumpled tissue in my hand and wiped my nose. "Do you have all your bags?"

"All ready to go." She patted her brand new piece of scarlet red luggage. Mark had bought it for her at the Flower Hill Mall on her last visit. At the time, we all joked that she wouldn't get too many opportunities to use it.

As I led Elizabeth outside toward the parking lot, late May's tepid night air soothed my nerves, a welcome contrast from the bone chilling air-conditioned corridors of the hospital and the belly of airport arrivals. "Mark's surgeries went really well. They set all his broken bones and his doctors told me they should heal nicely," I said, scanning the short-term parking for my silver Mercedes. "He's still on a ventilator and in a coma, but that's a good thing for the time being. It gives his body a chance to rest and heal."

"Has he shown any new signs he's going to be okay?" Elizabeth asked as I clicked off the car alarm and unlocked the doors.

"No." I tossed her luggage inside the safety of the trunk. "All we can do right now is wait."

***

Elizabeth found him laid out on one of the many beds in the Intensive Care Unit. I tried my best to give her privacy in the cramped, curtained off space. As she looked over her son, her eyes watered and her lips quivered.

Thin strips of white tape covered Mark's eyes. A large tube ran from his throat, connecting him to the ventilator. More tubes ran from his groin, arms, and neck. Computers bleeped, muffled voices squawked orders over the PA, and nurses chatted in hushed voices at the main station in the middle of the room.

Lying there in that dim, cramped section of the ICU, Mark's bloated and battered body looked more like a corpse than the healthy, handsome man Elizabeth had hugged goodbye only months ago.

Silent tears broke, slipping down her pale cheeks. My mother-in-law ran a finger over his forehead, pursing her lips at his freshly shaved head. Staples held together the long u-shaped gash running along the side of his left temple.

Smoothing out the thick beige blankets that warmed his body, I motioned to the two padded chairs by Mark's bedside. "Let's take a seat over here. The one with the permanent sag in the middle is all mine." I attempted a smile.

Elizabeth didn't respond. She stood over Mark's hospital bed, her shoulders shaking as she sobbed. I took a seat and waited for her to join me. She was a proud Southern woman, and I imagined this loss of control over her son's fate, as well as her own emotions, inflicted extra pain. I wrung my hands and listened to the whoosh of rubber-bottomed nurses' shoes walking the fake wood floor. When Elizabeth's tears ran dry, she sat in the hospital chair and spoke in a hushed tone under the loud rush of the ventilator and beeping monitors.

"Thank you for taking care of him for us."

"Of course," I replied, "he's my husband."

She brushed the side of her nose with her index finger. "When Mark was young, he was so skinny and uncoordinated. He tripped over his own feet one day on his way home from school. A dog scared him and he just stumbled and fell. Put his bottom teeth right through his lower lip and gave himself a concussion." She reached up and took hold of Mark's limp hand in hers while I held back fresh tears.

"When he came to, he had wet his pants and needed stitches on his lower lip. That's how he got that little scar there." She pointed to a splotch of skin on his swollen, expressionless face. "He came creeping through the front door trying to hide the blood and soiled pants from me. He was just so prone to accidents as a kid. From then on, I would work myself into a fit if he came home from school more than a few minutes late." Elizabeth kneaded the back of her neck.

I had my own memories. "You should have seen him on our first date. I agreed to meet him at Jamie's dorm. He showed up twenty minutes early with his curly brown hair slicked back and a dozen long stemmed roses in his hand." At the time, I could hardly believe the cocky frat boy I'd met at a kegger party had gone to the trouble of cleaning himself up and buying me flowers. "I didn't even have a vase to put them in. Jamie lent me one of her big plastic San Diego State cups." I smiled and looked at the ground. "When he put his mind to it, your son knew how to charm a girl.

If he were awake right now, he'd know just what to say to make us feel better." I warmed at the thought of it. "Another time back in college, soon after we started dating, Mark got stuck in traffic driving home from LA. He was supposed to come visit me." I looked over at him with the ridiculous hope he would chime in to finish one of my favorite stories.

"Anyway, we'd only been dating for about a month or so and he'd promised to check out my new apartment when he got back into town. My roommates were both out of town for the weekend, and he said he would be there at nine the latest.

Let me tell you, I went a little nuts that day. I cleaned that shabby little apartment from top to bottom, washed the sheets, did the dishes, changed my outfit at least three times before settling on an old pair of jeans and a T-shirt. Everything was just right for him. So of course he was late. When he finally called me at a quarter till ten and said they'd closed down three of the lanes on the 405 and he'd be at least another hour, I was beyond furious. I suggested he skip coming over altogether I was so mad at him."

"Why? He couldn't control traffic." Elizabeth interrupted my story.

"I don't know. I think it scared me that I cared so much whether he showed up or not. He was the so-called 'player frat boy' and I had such a guard up with him. I needed to keep myself from finding him too charming or necessary in my life. That way it wouldn't hurt so much if it didn't work out." I twisted the ring on my finger. "Anyway, he apologized profusely for not calling sooner, but I was inconsolable. I told him if he wanted to come over, I wasn't going to speak to him."

Elizabeth looked at me with her eyes narrowed in

what I hoped was mock exasperation. "So, what did he do?"

"He said 'OK' like it was no big deal and then he kind of chuckled, which made me even more angry. I asked him what was so funny and he said, 'It's stupid, but I'm glad you're mad at me for running late. It means you like me.' He intuitively understood my brand of crazy. That touched me."

I scooted my chair even closer to his bed, ready to share the best part of my story. "When he finally showed up at my place more than two hours late, my hair had gone flat and I had given up on keeping the apartment clean. I let him in through the security door, and he tried to give me a big hug right there in the lobby. I shrugged him off and reminded him I wasn't speaking to him. He said 'OK' again without any hint of frustration and followed me back up to my place.

When we got there, I had music playing on my CD player. He listened for a minute and then he walked over to me."

I gazed at Mark resting motionless in his hospital bed to see if there was the slightest indication on his face that he was registering any of this. He lie passive as I ran my fingers across the cool metal bar that kept him contained on the bed, but that was ok. It was such a beautiful memory. I could savor it for the both of us. Turning back toward Elizabeth, I continued. "So the music is playing. One of my all time favorites, The Fugees, *Killing Me Softly*. He took my hand and spoke into my ear, 'We don't have to talk, but can I dance with you?'"

I could hear all the lyrics swaying in my head. I was back there in my old apartment, slow dancing with my future husband. Butterflies were fluttering in my tummy, our possibilities were endless.

Then came reality. I was sitting in a cold Intensive Care Unit next to my grieving mother-in-law and near lifeless husband. I finished my story. "By the time the song finished, my exasperation evaporated."

He had kissed me on lips after that, so good it gave me the shivers. I knew right then I was in deep. He got me. He didn't take my irrational bad mood seriously, and he knew just how to fix it, in the most romantic way possible. We had made love that night and that was it. I couldn't imagine being with any other man ever again. I was his.

***

Weeks passed, spring turned to summer, and nothing changed. A small team of medical experts swept in and out of his room on regular, dependable shifts. I grew fond of his constant caretakers, especially Kate, his full-time day nurse. With her petite athletic body and light freckled nose, Kate felt familiar to me, as if we were old high school buddies. She looked after my husband as if he were family, monitoring his charts and medical devices with precision, patting him on the arm and telling him he was doing great even though he didn't respond. I was grateful to have her on our team.

Day and night we took turns keeping our vigil, waiting for any sign Mark would come back to us.

SAMANTHA: THURSDAY, JUNE 19

Cameron came home late again. He said he had some papers he needed to grade for his summer school class and it would be easier to get his work done at the office. His story made me think of that home wrecking whore he was surely having an affair with. My original plan to lay low and keep my cool was about to blow up in my face. I couldn't hold it in any longer.

He found me in bed rereading the opening scene from *The Lover* by Marguerite Duras. It was a devastating and brutal story of a wealthy man seducing a much younger woman who goes out of her way to capture his attention.

"Hey Sam, what are you doing awake?" Cameron asked, setting down his briefcase near our bedside table.

I watched him shove his hands into the pockets of

his designer black denim jeans. "You look guilty." I laid down my novel face up so he could see the cover.

"Excuse me?" His mouth gaped open while his brown eyes widened.

I smirked. Cameron was a terrible liar. The last time he went on a shopping spree for new clothes, he tried to hide the bags in the back of our closet. For the entire week, he looked as nervous as a straight-A-school-girl ditching fifth period algebra for the first time.

He headed toward our master bathroom, talking to me as he tramped away. "Okay Sam. Have it your way. I plead the fifth. I don't know what you're talking about."

"Taking a shower? Washing her scent off before you come to bed with your wife, the mother of your *three* children? That's kind of you Cameron." I kept my voice even, desperate for him to prove me wrong.

"I'm taking a shower to wash off the day." He turned on the water and unbuttoned his pants. "Jesus Samantha, what's gotten into you? Spending too much free time with the gossips of Kingston Court? They putting scandalous ideas in your head?"

"Not exactly Cameron. You've been coming home late most nights for a month now. You've been more careful about what you wear to class. You're distracted." I watched his reflection in the mirror, waiting for his rebuttal.

Cameron opened the glass shower door and

stepped inside. Water shifted its course, pelting his body rather than the mosaic-tiled floor. He was hiding from me, washing away the evidence. My stomach turned and I felt like throwing up.

He wasn't home on time to tuck our six-year-old son into bed. Our teenage daughters Sophia and Savanna had questions on their homework that went unanswered.

Rage swept through my body. Instantly, I was ten years old again, coming home from school with a note for the father-daughter dance, tearing it in thirds and dumping it in the trash. I didn't have a dad. He had left my mother and me without even bothering to hug us goodbye.

I grew up in a small, conservative town where little girls without daddies were not-so-secretly pitied and looked down upon with suspicion. Suzy homemakers thought my mother was on the hunt to steal their lousy husbands. I was a dirty girl, treated like a bad influence on the kids from good families. My father did that to us.

This man was not getting off the hook so easily. I stomped out of bed and stormed into the steaming bathroom, the mirror covered in a thick fog. "You son of a bitch! You fucking little coward whore! How could you do this to us?" I smacked the shower door. "And for what? For some young piece of ass you'll forget about in a month's time, maybe less."

He scrubbed shampoo into his hair. Peppermint and sage mist filled the air. "Calm down, Samantha.

Nothing happened. There's no girl." He closed his eyes and leaned the back of his head under the spray.

I punched the glass door again, this time with the side of my fist, making it shake.

"Good lord. You're going to break the damn thing."

"Screw the door. You could at least be honest. Own up to it like a man."

Cameron lifted his sculpted arm, his back to the nozzle, and rinsed his thick brown mane. Aside from a couple of deep frown lines between his brows, he looked better than the day I married him. The bastard was aging in reverse.

I ran a hand over my own hipbones, touching the C-section scars marked across my pubic region. Stretch marks tracked along my once irresistible breasts and tiny pockets of back fat clung behind my hips, refusing to dissolve no matter how hard I worked out. Three pregnancies had diminished my figure. At forty-one, I could never compete with a twenty-year-old. No amount of plastic surgery or strenuous exercise would enable me to keep up with the fresh meat that packed his classroom every new semester. I went back to bed and fumed.

Cameron joined me when he was ready. The heat of his naked body warmed my backside. "Sam," he whispered, kissing my shoulder. "I love you. There's no other woman besides you. I swear to God." He ran his long elegant fingers through my hair. My body responded, wanting him, needing him. He was mine. She had only borrowed a small piece of him.

I rolled toward him and stroked the contours of his chest. "Make love to me then."

His body stiffened. "It's late. This is ridiculous."

"If I'm being ridiculous then show me you love me. Prove it." I put my hand on his arm and grabbed him toward me, feeling a fresh wave of anger tighten my chest.

"I'm tired. Can we talk about this tomorrow? I love you. Okay? You're the only woman I love."

Crushed, I turned over and let the angry tears slide down my face.

NATALIE: FRIDAY AFTERNOON
JUNE 20

Mark opened his eyes. Four long weeks after the accident, just after Mark's dad left San Diego to go back to work, Mark's eyes fluttered open and then shut.

It was my shift. Elizabeth was home with the kids. Kate gave me a look that seemed to say, "Wait."

My heart bounced into my solar plexus, sucking away my breath. This was the new beginning we had been waiting for. This was the moment that would predict all that came next.

Mark opened his eyes again and blinked a few times, looking around in a daze. Kate spoke to him in her typical calm, comforting tone. "Mark, everything is okay. My name is Kate. I'm your ICU nurse." He pushed his head back into his pillow and furrowed his brows. My husband looked stunned and disoriented. I wanted to touch him but I was afraid to move.

"You're at California General Hospital in La Jolla. Your wife Natalie is here." Kate glanced over at me and motioned for me to step forward.

"Go ahead and hold his hand," she said. "He is probably very confused right now. He's coming out of a deep sleep and he may not recognize you, but you can still reassure him that he is in safe hands."

Nodding my head, I made the single step toward his bedside as if I were moving through a thick suffocating fog. I had rehearsed this moment in my head every night since the accident.

Now that it was really happening, I had to fight to stay present. A part of me wanted to pick up my cell phone and tell everyone we loved that Mark was awake, that he was going to be all right. Another piece of me wanted to put my hands on some old analog clock and suspend time.

I took a timid step forward.

"Mark?"

NATALIE: FRIDAY AFTERNOON
JUNE 20

Mark and I didn't have a flawless marriage. Who did? I wanted babies right away. He was, despite his age, an only child at heart, and he worried he would lose my attention, that a demanding infant would change our relationship for the worse.

Mark worked longer hours after Lana was born and picked stupid fights when I tried to leave the house without her for short periods of time. *Did I really need to go to the gym that evening? Was it so important to see a girlfriend in person I had just spoke to on the phone the other day?* I resented his lack of interest in helping me out with our baby but was too caught up in my new role as a mommy to do much about it.

When Lana learned to walk and talk, father and

daughter bonded. Then came Ben. For the first four months he cried day and night. He wouldn't sleep for more than a few hours at a time until he was nearly a year old. Every mother had her challenges, and Ben was mine.

Mark conveniently enrolled in graduate school, took on a promotion at work, and just as he did when Lana was born, pulled away from us. I considered leaving him, but I loved him, and I figured I was better off living like a single mom with the benefit of my husband's full income and occasional help, rather than actually being completely on my own raising two young kids.

So I stayed.

Ben grew older and while he was still prone to temper tantrums and frustrating obsessions, like brushing his teeth after every meal with his green toothbrush, he became easier. Mark wrapped up his MBA program and slipped back into our lives. Once again, he ate dinners with us and played with the kids before bedtime. He brought home bouquets of my favorite flowers and asked me out on romantic dates. Mark made me feel loved again and there were days I counted the minutes until he came home from work. I took extra pride in our relationship. We had grown stronger for having made it through such a tough time. Now, just when I had my husband back, a drunk driver crashed into us and put him in a coma.

"Hon? It's me, your wife." I looked at him blinking

his eyes in his hospital bed. My mind gained traction. "We've all been waiting for you to wake up, sweetheart. Your family has missed you so much." He stared back at me like a startled child waking from a nightmare. "You were in a car accident. But you're okay now. The doctors and your wonderful nurse here, Kate, have been taking very good care of you."

His eyes closed. I spoke faster, desperate to reach him, draw him back out. We couldn't lose him again. "A guy ran his old SUV into our car and pushed us off the road. I know you might not remember a whole lot right now, but you will. You knocked your head around pretty good so it's going take some time for everything to come back to you." I squeezed his hand. "Mark? Can you open your eyes again?"

Doctors had taken him off the ventilator the previous week. Pushing his lips together, he opened and closed his mouth several times before clearing his throat. He might be preparing to tell me he loved me, or maybe he couldn't speak at all, couldn't remember language. On the other hand, maybe he would say he had been dreaming about me for days and it was my voice and stories that pulled him from the abyss.

"Is there something you want to say?" I lifted my eyebrows in hope.

He opened his eyes again and looked at me. I steeled myself for his reaction. "What is it?" I brushed my fingers across his bare cheek.

Again, he cleared his throat. "I," he shut his mouth

and then opened it again. "Wattter."

"Oh, of course, of course." I turned to his nurse. "Kate, can I get him something to drink. He's thirsty."

She nodded. "I already paged someone to bring ice chips. They'll be here soon."

I squeezed Mark's arm in excitement, fighting the urge to give Kate a high five. My husband had told us he was thirsty. It meant he could talk. "Honey, is there anything else you want to tell us?"

"Water." He closed his eyes and his face went slack.

I turned to Kate. "This is good right? I should call his mom?"

"Yes. That would be a great idea. You might want her to leave the kids at home though. Like we explained to you, it's as if Mark is coming out of a very deep sleep right now, he's going to need some time to become lucid, to be able to recognize faces. It might scare the kids to see their dad so disoriented. Especially since your little guy, Ben, has had such a hard time of it."

I nodded my head in excitement. "But it's a good sign that he is talking, right? You said he might not be able to speak when he first woke up."

She fiddled with the edge of her purple scrubs. "It means the damage done to his brain is not in the part of his head that controls speech."

I let go of my husband's hand and wrapped my arms around his nurse. "You have been so good to our family throughout this whole ordeal. I don't know what we would have done without you. We owe you the world."

"You have a great family." She smiled. "Besides, Mark's been an easy patient, real quiet and polite."

I laughed at her joke. "It takes a lot to shut that man up."

She tilted her head, her gentle green eyes peering from her freckled face. "You better call Elizabeth. She'll never forgive you if you keep her waiting."

"No kidding." I dug my phone out from the bottom of my bag. Dialing with care, my fingers trembled as I tapped each number and paced the small curtained off space, waiting for my mother-in-law to answer. "Elizabeth? He opened his eyes. He spoke." Tears of relief and joy slid down my cheeks. "Just now."

***

Mark's mom left the kids with Jamie and made it to the hospital so fast she could have caused her own car wreck.

"Where is he?" she asked, rushing through the automatic double doors and pushing through the curtains. "Where's my boy?"

I stepped back to give her some space. As much as I wanted to dominate Mark's attention, I knew Elizabeth needed him too.

He looked at her stressed face and thick mane of

severe black hair and squinted his eyes with a glimmer of recognition, something he hadn't done for me. "Mark, how are you feeling my love?" she asked.

"Goooood," he slurred it out slow as if the word was one long sentence. It was the only word he had spoken since I'd given him ice chips.

"That is just wonderful. You gave us a real scare these past few weeks, son." She leaned in closer and kissed his forehead. "Don't you ever do that again, you hear?" Elizabeth used the side of her finger to wipe away a fat tear rolling down her cheek.

"Mom?" he asked, staring at her face in wonder.

"Yes, I'm your mother. That woman over there," she pointed to me with a tight smile, "she's your wife, Natalie. Your father and Natalie have been here with me all along waiting for you to wake up. Your daytime nurse Kate, is here too. We've all been taking real good care of you. You're going to be up and running before you know it."

New footsteps. A tall, slender man with thinning blond hair and patient eyes walked through the wide gap in the curtains. Dr. Cohen was my favorite doctor in the ICU. He always took the time to speak to me like a woman concerned for her comatose husband rather than another high-maintenance family member on his check-off list.

The tight knots in my neck and shoulders loosened at the sight of him. Dr. Cohen would sort this all out. Any moment now, Mark would look at me the way he looked at his mother, with a sense of recognition.

Elizabeth and I hovered close to Mark and waited as Kate gave the doctor a full update.

"Ladies, do you mind if I ask Mark a few questions?"

"Of course not." Elizabeth and I spoke in unison, both of us standing in place like frightened children, unwilling or unable to move.

My adrenaline kicked in again. The room shrunk, my head buzzed with suffocating fear. Dr. Cohen pulled up a stool and wheeled close to Mark's bedside. "Hello, there. I'm Dr. Ari Cohen." He spoke in a soft, gentle voice. "How are you doing?"

I craned my neck to watch for my husband's response. Mark looked back at his doctor without speaking.

"Listen, we're going to run you through a series of small tests to see where you're at. Nurse Kate tells me you've been swallowing. That's very good news."

Dr. Cohen tugged on his stethoscope. "Do you know where you are Mark?"

Kate looked at her charts while Elizabeth and I leaned forward, waiting in anticipation for Mark's answer. We had told him where he was, would he remember?

With his eyes closed, Mark answered the question, "Hosssspital." We all smiled in relief, his short term memory seemed to be intact.

"Excellent. That's right, you are here at California

General Hospital in La Jolla. Do you know *why* you are here?"

I rubbed my hand across my heart. Mark opened his eyes, looked at the doctor and then over at his mom and me. "Hurt."

"Great, just a few more questions. Do you know what year it is?"

"2000?"

Dr. Cohen smiled at Mark's answer. "June, 2014, but you're close. Do you know your age?"

"No."

"According my charts, you're a hair over forty. How about this nice lady standing right here?" The doctor motioned toward Elizabeth. "Do you recognize her?"

Mark nodded. "Mom."

A hopeful smile spread into my cheeks as the doctor gestured to me. "And how about this woman here?"

Mark stared for a moment as I held my breath and wrapped my hands around the cool steel of his bed rail. Words had been a struggle for him, but I waited for my name. He blinked his eyes and shook his head.

My heart plummeted. "Mark. Sweetie." I bent down and reached for his hand, desperate to reunite. "It's me. Natalie." My voice, maybe my name, something had to jog his memory. "We met in college and we married just after I graduated. We have two children together, a girl and a boy. Lana and Ben.

He said nothing.

I hung my head to hide the flush of embarrassment. The doctors, Kate, the other nurses, they all warned me this could happen. They said every brain injury was different. Some patients might not be able to speak. Others might not be able to recognize objects. It was also quite common for someone to come out of a coma and not remember the people they loved the most.

Dark bloated clouds temporarily shrouded the sun, dimming the hospital room and turning the summer sky an ugly gray. I'd found myself in a cramped space full of strangers. They were all staring at me, including my husband. Mark eyed the doctor for reassurance.

Dr. Cohen pursed his lips. "It's normal not to remember everything when you first come out of a coma. Overall you are doing well Mark."

I took a few awkward steps backward. I adored my husband. He had wooed himself completely back into my heart this past year. We worked hard to get our marriage back, scheduling date nights, asking more questions about each other's daily routine and making time for sex at least once a week. I yearned for that close connection we'd built. We had children we needed to raise together. How could he recognize his mother, but not me?

Grabbing at my sweater with shaking hands and tugging it up over my head, I told myself he'd known his mom since birth so it made sense she looked vaguely familiar. I was not going to be jealous. He was awake. That was all that mattered. Still, that selfish ache for him to recognize me and our love felt tight in my chest.

Elizabeth took her son's hand and praised him, while I pulled Dr. Cohen outside the curtains. "What do you think? I understand it's a good sign that he is talking. Can we expect his memory to improve as well over the next few days? You know, I'm wondering what's best to do with our children. Maybe I should hold off on bringing them for a little while?" I wanted to sound brave, like the fact my husband didn't recognize me was not my top concern. I was a good wife and a good mother. I was worried about my children, that was all.

Dr. Cohen put his hand on my shoulder and gave me his complete attention. "Mark's health is improving, but only time will tell if he regains his full memory. Bring the kids in whenever you are ready."

"Thank you doctor." A hot tear rolled down my chin.

"Natalie, he is doing better than we first expected. But Mark still has a long journey ahead of him. Try to stay focused on the positives of each day."

Stepping back through the half mesh and half cotton hospital curtains, I pushed in next to Elizabeth and fought the urge to touch my husband. The two of us hovered there, me standing, Elizabeth sitting in the chair she had pulled over and holding his hand.

"Mark?" I clutched the bedrail. "Is it okay if I tell

you a little bit about Lana and Ben?"

He titled his head in our direction. "What happened to me?"

His response grounded me. Mark was disorientated, confused and probably in a lot of pain. Of course he wasn't interested in hearing about the children he didn't remember. He wanted to know what happened to *him*.

I tugged at a loose thread on my sleeve and prepared to answer his question. "We were driving downtown on a date night for my thirty-eighth birthday when we were hit by a drunk driver, some guy driving an SUV with a suspended license. He slammed into the driver's side of our car and flew through his windshield. The police said he wasn't wearing a seat belt and his airbag didn't go off. Dead on arrival." I shook my head, trying to feel a measure of sympathy for the man who had nearly killed my husband and stolen his memories. Instead I felt numb. Mark looked at me without much emotion, none that I could read anyway.

I pulled my seat next to him and sat down. "Your car rolled and you hit your head on the roof as we tumbled over and skidded into a lamp post. A couple of guys pulled us out when the fire started." I shivered at the thought of what could have happened to us both if those four men hadn't stepped up and taken action so quickly. "The good news is, I'm fine. Your broken bones and collapsed lung are almost healed, but your head got shaken up. That's why you don't remember me or our children yet. But please know," I reached out and touched his cheek, "we all love you so much."

He bit his lip in response and closed his eyes.

"Mark," I continued, grasping his shoulder. "Our daughter Lana is twelve. You help her with her insanely complicated math homework each night and coach her soccer team." Feeling his shoulder stiffen, I pulled my hand back, but kept talking. "Ben is five. He is a blond haired version of me—a big worry wart with lots of emotion. He is so eager to see you. We all miss you so much." I fought back a wave of tears.

If my husband didn't remember meeting me, did that mean he might not love me again? Would he feel a bond with his children? Would he even want to come home or would he prefer to live on his own?

Every piece of me yearned for my happy ending.

SAMANTHA: THURSDAY EVENING,
JUNE 26

Gathered beneath the sculpted palm trees of Jamie's well manicured front yard, we lounged in garden chairs and drank red wine while we watched our kids zip around Kingston Court's private streets on skateboards and trikes. It was one of those particularly ideal Southern California evenings. The sunset painted pink and purple watercolor splashes across the waning sky. The temperature hovered around seventy degrees.

I may have been persona non-grata as far as my husband and oldest daughter were concerned, but my girlfriends in the neighborhood still fawned over me like a celebrity. They kept an eye on my kids when they ventured outside, complimented the fresh flowers blooming in my garden, and made sure I joined them every Thursday for drinks in the cul-de-sac.

Natalie Delisse, a mousey stay-at-home mom who bought a house right next door to her very best friend from college, rarely missed a night. She was one of those "perfect" moms. The type who made a big deal about volunteering three days a week at the elementary school and hand painted obnoxious sun-shiny signs for her children's lemonade stands. She never really added much to any conversation, but this evening was different. Natalie and her bestie Jamie droned on and on about Natalie's husband. We spent at least half an hour discussing their car crash and Mark's recovery process. I felt awful for both of them, but I was also a little freaked out about the whole thing and ready to talk about something else.

The other women got sucked into it all. Their mouths gaped open and their eyes stayed wide with the look of horror and fear that it could happen to any of us. I chose to zone out and listen for the crash of the waves from the nearby ocean, to breath in the salty air. It was important to keep centered.

I was patting out a drop of spilled wine on my expensive boho ivory shift dress when Marina, the queen of gossip, sauntered over smiling like a woman who just scored the best deal of her life at the Nordstrom's Anniversary Sale. Eyeing her with great interest, I decided if Marina told us something good, I might consider forgiving her for what I overheard her whispering about Cameron and me the other day, about us getting into an argument over Sophia in the driveway. Marina knew everything that went on within a ten mile radius. It was best to play nice with her.

Marina pushed her feral blond ringlets off her face as the ladies greeted her. She grinned even wider, every line on her forehead begging for Botox. Now I knew she had something juicy to tell us.

"Has anyone seen Nora lately? I heard she left, but that can't be true, can it?"

Beth, one of our nerdy neighbors who loved hanging out with us, cleared her throat and looked around for our reaction. Her tan shorts bulged in the butt and thighs, and I watched in irritation as she pulled her thick white sports socks higher up her calf. She looked more like a lesbian soccer coach than a stay-at-home mom living in a wealthy beachside community.

"I noticed she isn't around much," I volunteered, eager to cut Beth off before she said something stupid and steered the conversation away from Marina's gossip.

Jess, my closest friend on Kingston Court, threw in her two cents. "I haven't seen Nora either, now that you mention it." She stuck out her lower lip in a dramatic pout. "Poor Jason is out almost every evening pulling their kids around in that little red wagon. He looks exhausted."

Beth bobbed her head up and down in wild agreement like she had some sort of social disorder. "Jason loves those kids. They are so adorable."

Jason Ellis toted his two little children around the neighborhood like he actually enjoyed it. Nora, his ball busting wife with Ivy League credentials, brought home the big bucks. She went off to work and Jason did everything else. Their whole relationship felt tragic. How could a wife respect a man who changed diapers all day long? It just wasn't sexy.

I was preparing to tell Marina to spill it when I noticed Natalie averting her puppy dog brown eyes to the ground. She was friends with Nora and by the look of tension pinching her forehead and tightening her jawline, I was certain she knew something.

Swirling the blood-red liquid in my glass, I raised an eyebrow at her. "Seems like someone has some information they'd like to share." I smiled.

Marina jumped right in. "Well, I heard Nora left a note." She paused for added drama. "Packed her bags while the rest of the family was out for the day and disappeared. She typed up a letter on Jason's laptop saying she needed some time off. Can you imagine?"

The other ladies gasped. Jess spoke first, her soft pink lips parted in shock. "She left her children?"

"Yep," Marina confirmed. "Left them with Jason and not even a phone call since."

"Guess it doesn't pay to be a house husband," I heard myself say out loud. It was catty and mean spirited. Worst of all, it made me a hypocrite. Jason's plight could be my own story if I didn't play my cards right. For all I knew, Cameron was hunched over somewhere writing me a goodbye note right this second, preparing to leave me behind to raise our children on my own.

I nudged Marina for more details. "Why did she leave him? Did the note say anything else?"

Natalie cleared her throat and sat up straighter. The move added a couple of inches to her tiny five-foot-nothing frame. From her seated position, she could actually stare me down from eye level. "Nora said she was going to Guam. She's staying with her family there. She needed some time to think." Natalie pursed her lips before continuing. "Nora left Jason with full control of her trust fund. She didn't abandon her children. She just needed a break. Motherhood isn't for everyone." Natalie raised her glass to her mouth and took a sip, glaring at me as if to say, "Conversation over."

Well it wasn't over for me. Not by a long shot. I didn't give a damn if Nora left her family millions, she still abandoned them. "Leaving them a blank check doesn't excuse her behavior. It doesn't erase the pain she's inflicting on Grace and little what's-his-name." Nora's disappearance felt personal, as if I was the one being left behind.

"Their names are Grace and Andrew. No one is perfect, Samantha." Natalie shot back, her eyes focused on the sidewalk.

Heat spread across my neck. I wanted to scream. Natalie reminded me of the quintessentially goodygood girl-next-door who saw the best in everyone.

She just didn't get it. Life was black and white. No in-between. Natalie's insistence on seeing everything in fifty shades of gray pissed me off. A parent should not abandon their children. No exceptions.

"*Perfect*? No one is *perfect*?" I tucked a stray hair behind my ear and fought to maintain my civility in front of our friends, especially considering Natalie's own recent tragedy. "On what planet is tossing aside your spouse and children a minor faux pas? I suppose it was an accident. She'll be back next week with an apology? *Oops, so sorry about that. I didn't mean to treat my family like yesterday's garbage. I really do love you and want to dedicate my life to you.* Give me a break."

"It doesn't mean she doesn't love them," Natalie said in a lowered, steady voice.

"It means she doesn't love them *enough*."

Natalie stared hard at the ground, probably too intimidated to make direct eye contact. "I think this is none of our business. Shit happens. Nora left Grace and Andrew in the care of their fully capable father and she gave them her life's savings. Who are you to judge?"

All my friends besides clueless Beth shifted their body weight in my direction, an obvious sign of their allegiance.

"Of course I can have an opinion. These are our neighbors. Their children play with our children. You don't think this will affect us all?" I turned to Beth. "Do you feel safe with your only daughter playing with Nora's kids? How would Liora feel if she knew you could leave her?"

Jamie, Natalie's only true ally, sneered at me. "You better watch it Samantha."

I stared back at her, daring her to take it a step further.

"I hear Shelby crying inside." Jamie's nostrils flared ever so slightly. "Natalie, will you help me check on her?"

Graced with porcelain skin and Kewpie doll bow shaped lips, Jamie, with her peroxide blonde hair, was the only woman in the neighborhood who came close to matching my good looks. I couldn't stand her.

"Sure," Natalie agreed with her bff, still staring at her own feet, incapable of looking me directly in the eye. "I could use a breather." She stood and snuck away through Jamie's mahogany front door.

My chest burned in anger. I glared at Jamie's empty porch, laced with pink bougainvillea and perfectly placed bright potted plants. Kingston Court only gave the appearance of tranquility, the truth was not so pretty. What was Natalie thinking? How could anyone defend such inexcusable behavior?

Jess giggled. Her overly augmented boobs threatened to break free from her sundress. Did she really need that much attention?

"Wow," Jess said, oblivious to me eying up her silicon stuffed chest. "Someone was a little overprotective.

Jeez, a mom flies off to Guam, and we're all okay with that?"

"Soars off to a foreign country with nothing more than a note saying she may or may not be back," I added, happy for the support.

The ladies and I continued our drinking and conversation until the moon shined as bright as the streetlights and our children were actually begging to go inside. Walking back to our respective homes, a pang of guilt stabbed at me, making me feel the need to apologize for my outburst with Natalie. She wasn't such a bad person. I actually kind of respected her instinct to protect a friend.

All the same, her story struck a real nerve. Mark's car crash and Nora's fly-by-night escape left me feeling even more vulnerable than I had before. I refused to be the next person in the neighborhood to find herself alone.

SAMANTHA: TUESDAY EVENING
JULY 1

I boarded my flight to Portland with a small overnight bag and a newfound confidence. No more feeling second best. I was confronting my fears head on.

Cameron left last night for a supposed academic conference. I told Jess I wanted to surprise him with a passionate night alone and showed her the new white lace lingerie I was taking with me. She loved the idea and agreed to take all three of my kids for a sleepover at her place.

With a quick phone call, I had already verified Cameron's exact location. He was staying at some generic mid-priced hotel that offered a questionable swimming pool and a continental breakfast in the lobby each morning. According to Google Images, there was no back door on any of the rooms for a guilty lover to escape. I would rent a car when the plane landed, drive straight to his hotel, knock on the door, and insist he answer.

The jet engine roared at takeoff, pushing us all back in our seats. I tightened my lap belt and plugged my nose, trying to clear my ears before they filled with painful pressure.

The irony that my marriage could come to blows in Portland was not lost on me. It was the city my father had moved to before completely severing ties with my mom and me. It's where he built a new family and discarded us for good.

Toward the end of the flight, I pulled out my handbag and touched up my lipstick. The flight attendant stopped by to pick up any last minute trash and make sure all tray tables were up. I told myself Portland was just another place, another overcast town with too much rain. Whatever happened here, it could be fixed and forgotten. I had no intention of losing my husband to some frivolous fling.

A rectangular sign, glowing a dim orange in the darkened cabin, reminded us to keep our belts fastened a little longer. I pushed up the window cover and put my seat in the upright position, looking out at an inky night sky and waiting for impact.

The drive to the hotel was easy. Traffic was minimal and my directions were dead on. Thanks to the clueless receptionist who gave me his room number, I knocked on Cameron's door somewhere around nine o'clock. From the other side of the bolted door, a low voice asked a muffled question and then a voice that sounded like Cameron's stammered out something in return.

Shifting the weight from my left leg to the right and wrapping my bare arms around myself to ward off the chill settling into the night air, I bit hard into the tip of my tongue.

"Can I help you?" Cameron asked through the closed door.

I had briefly contemplated responding to this very question in a high-pitched voice, claiming to be the housekeeping service. Realizing this was an undignified approach, I opted for the truth.

"Cameron, it's Samantha. Your wife."

A man in a cheap business suit scooted behind me in the narrow outdoor breezeway. He gave me a nod with a stiff polite smile. I could practically hear him thinking that some poor sucker was about to get caught.

"Sam?"

"Yes."

"What are you doing here?" Cameron asked.

I set down my Anthropology overnight bag. "Perhaps this conversation would be easier if you opened the door." I doubted that was completely true. Judging by his hesitation, Cameron was weighing his options. None of them were going to be easy.

I heard some rustling around and then the latch unlocked. The air inside his hotel room smelled musky and damp. A small knot in my lower back stiffened.

"Sam, I wish you wouldn't have come here."

Dressed in a familiar pair of dark, fitted jeans along with a tight San Diego Padres T-shirt I didn't recognize, Cameron looked at me like he had just been told his mother didn't love him anymore.

His sadness came as a surprise and I forgot whatever lines I had rehearsed.

"Come inside." He opened the door wider.

I dropped my purse and bag on the floor by the door and sat on the edge of a rigid chair, facing his rumpled queen sized bed. "Looks like you have company," I said, eyeing the discarded pillows and lonely comforter abandoned on the floor.

He sat on the naked mattress and looked back at me. "This isn't how I wanted to tell you."

"How did you want to tell me?"

A tear slipped down my cheek and I knew ugly red splotches were forming on my neck. Coming here was a mistake. I wasn't ready to hear whatever it was he had to say.

"I didn't." He cleared his throat. "I didn't have a plan. I'm glad you came though, Sam. I swear, keeping this secret from you was going to give me cancer. You're my best friend and I've felt so alone in this."

I bit my lip. Cameron's crumpled face and slumped shoulders reminded me of a broken Ken doll. This wasn't how it was supposed to go down. I expected to catch him in the act. The girl would hang her head in humiliation and Cameron would beg for my forgiveness. He would promise to put everything right. In my worst case scenario, the woman wouldn't back down and Cameron would claim to be in love with her. He'd tell me that the two of us were over and I would have to set aside my pride and convince him to change his mind.

This, whatever this was, was far worse.

"What's going on Cameron?"

He placed his hands on his lap and looked at me. "I'm gay."

"Don't fuck with me. You think this is funny? You think this makes it better?" I stood from my chair. "Where is she?" I charged at the bathroom door ready for a full blown war. I twisted the handle, and sure enough, it was locked. "Open the goddamned door you little slut." I kicked at the cheap plywood blocking my path, too numb to feel the force against my toes. "Open the fucking door!"

The air pressure in the room thundered in my eardrums. Why was he doing this to me? Why was I doing this to myself? I felt like lighting the place on fire.

"You can come out, David," Cameron said, coming up behind me and putting a hand on my trembling shoulder. "It's okay."

The door opened.

A handsome young boy, college age, in boxers and nothing more, stood facing me with his eyes cast to the floor. With his tousled dark brown hair and trim build, he looked like a twenty-year-old version of our son Gavin. "Sorry ma'am," he said, rubbing salt to the wound.

My husband's lover called me ma'am.

"You dirty fucker," I glared at Cameron. "I hope whoever was in charge here wore a condom."

He shook his head. "That's what I love about you, Sam. You always have your priorities straight."

I pushed past them both and slammed the battered door, shutting them out behind me. Dry heaving into the bathtub, I assured myself this was not happening. I was slipping down the rabbit hole. This had to be some altered reality. I placed my forehead on the rim of the cool porcelain tub, hoping it would soothe the pounding in my head or at the very least ease my trembling.

Earlier on in our marriage, I did a search through our internet history and found sites for gay porn. When I mentioned it to Cameron he acted clueless. Dozens of times in the past year, Cameron had led me to believe he was one place, only to find out he hadn't been there at all. He never flirted with my girlfriends, or turned his head when a pretty girl walked by. So many signs I had written off or ignored. I had told myself the porn must have been an accident. Who would want to admit they clicked the wrong button and ended up on an ass-fucking website? He loved and respected me too much to ever show interest in other women.

How could I have been so stupid? How was he able to have sex with me three times a week? I couldn't even imagine making love to a woman on a regular basis and pretending I liked it. Once or twice sure, but for all of these years? I felt a sliver of hope. Maybe Cameron was bisexual.

After touching up my smudged mascara and running a comb through my hair, I mustered the courage to walk out of the bathroom. His lover had already made a swift exit.

I looked at Cameron sitting on the bed, his head hung in shame. "How long has this been going on?" I asked, crossing my arms while standing over him and waiting for an answer.

"With David? I met him a few semesters ago, but this," he waved his hand around the room alluding to his affair. "This hasn't been going on for long."

I didn't believe him. "How long have you known you wanted to fuck men?"

"I didn't set out to deceive you Sam. I wanted you. I loved you from the beginning. You were everything I hoped for in a woman."

"In a woman," I deadpanned. "But you didn't want a woman."

"I wanted you. I knew if it could work with anyone, it would be you." He looked up at me with genuine affection. "You could stop a room with your smile. I really do love you. You're passionate and opinionated, and I always have fun with you. I've done a good job as a husband, haven't I?"

So he wasn't bisexual. He'd been faking it all along, trying to make both of us believe it was true. "You used me." I began to pace the room. "This is like every cliché in the book. You're good looking, kind, intelligent, love children. You worshipped the beautiful, well dressed blonde any straight man would desire."

Cameron patted the space beside him, but I ignored his invitation.

Pushing the hair out of my eyes, I continued my pacing. "I should have known."

"How could you have guessed? I couldn't even admit it to myself. This isn't what I wanted. I didn't choose to be this way."

When I met Cameron at that bar in San Francisco twenty years ago, I was out on the dance floor letting off some steam, enjoying the attention of the hot guys who frequented the place. I was a recent college dropout with no clear plan for my future. Cameron was a tall, handsome, eligible guy, full of confidence and dressed in expensive clothes. He was two years older than me and had just begun his first year at Stanford grad school.

He was everything I had ever hoped for—a man who put me on a pedestal and worshipped me. I was his princess and he was the real deal, my honest to goodness, I'll-never-leave-you-in-the-middle-of-the-night-for-something-better, Prince Charming.

Of course he was gay. How could I have not seen it?

Another wave of sadness thawed my anger. I collapsed down on the bed next to him, sitting my body close to his. "Why is this happening Cameron? I don't deserve this," I said, wishing he was mine again. "All the good ones are taken or gay, right? I was the perfect beard."

"You weren't a beard."

"I was. I was the ideal woman your oh-so-important family would accept and that you could tolerate as a life partner—the next best thing to a penis."

His warm breath caressed the top of my head as he rubbed my back. "That first time I saw you, I fell in love with you. I knew you were the only woman I could ever be with. That's why I pursued you the way I did. There was no need to look around, or think things over. You were the only one. I wanted the life I could make with you."

"God, Cameron," I laced my fingers through his, craving the familiar touch of his soft hand. "I want to hate you right now."

My husband wrapped a comforting arm around me like he often did when I needed him most. I tried to ignore the thoughts racing through my head, the ones that asked how I was going to manage three kids on my own. How would it feel not to wait for Cameron to come home from work or to sit without him at family dinners?

I was a fragile, shattered child, who had just lost her very best friend. Cameron held me close and let me weep in his arms. I was going to end up like my mother—alone.

NATALIE: WEDNESDAY, JULY 2

I sat on the porch steps of Jamie's front yard pulling crinkly pink petals off a fallen bougainvillea. Our little ones colored the warm asphalt streets with pastel chalk. Lana, my twelve-year-old going on twenty-two, watched over the younger kids, playing protective mommy.

Beth and her daughter Liora jaunted by. "Hi ladies." She waved both her hands with great enthusiasm. "How are Jamie and Natalie today?" she practically yelled.

I smiled, hoping she wouldn't join us. I needed to talk with Jamie in private.

"Li Li and I have a play date this afternoon. Li Li, tell Jamie and Natalie what we are doing today. Tell them what you're going to do."

Liora, the same age as my Ben, tucked her head in embarrassment and buried her face in her mother's soft hip. "I'm going to my friend Jessica's," she mumbled.

Beth nodded her head up and down so hard I worried she might injure herself. "And tell them what you are going to do there."

"Play."

"Very good Li Li. Smart girl. Okay then, we better prepare for our little outing. After that we'll be returning to the homestead." Beth clearly loved her daughter, but she treated Liora more like an anxious pet she didn't quite know what to with than an actual human being. Last summer when Liora fell from a tree and sprained her wrist, Beth was so rattled she called 911.

As Jamie fiddled with the strap on her Espadrille, Beth took her daughter by the hand. "I'll see my two favorite Kingston Court gal pals soon. Gooooodbye ladiesss," she sing-songed.

"Bye." Jamie and I waved in relief.

An emerald green hummingbird hovered over a nearby patch of lavender. Jamie scrunched her wide, thoughtful eyes in the balmy afternoon sunshine.

"So…" I wrapped my arms around my bent knees. "Mark is moving into rehab next week, which is great, but the doctors say he could be there for up to a year working on his recovery."

"Do they really think it could take that long?"

"Yes."

"But he's talking and he recognizes his parents."

"I know, I thought it might be a couple of months, but a whole year away from his home? How is he going to get to know us again if he isn't around to tuck the kids into bed or fall asleep with me at night. No reading books with Lana or sword fighting with Ben.

Plus, if he can't go back to work, I need to figure out how I'm going to pay the bills. Disability isn't going to cover all the expenses."

Ben, who was drawing smiley faces with Jamie's three-year-old daughter, waved to us from the cul-de-sac. We both waved back. I wished I could trade places with her carefree daughter for just one day.

"I keep running the options through my head and no matter what I come up with, I feel guilty."

Jamie nodded in understanding.

"I want to be there for Mark every day, but I also need to keep the water running and the lights on. We don't have enough in our savings to cover costs for more than a month or two. A part of me thinks we should just sell our house."

"What?"

"Where else am I going to get that kind of money?"

Jamie crossed her legs and looked me in the eyes. I waited for her sage advice.

"First off," she flicked a small bug off her thigh, "selling a house and finding a new place to live takes time. Second of all, you'd be uprooting Lana and Ben right after their dad went away, not to mention leaving the support of your best friend right next door. Moving is not a good option."

I buried my face in my hands, feeling the beginnings of yet another searing headache. Jamie wasn't helping. "So I keep the house, find a full time job, take care of the kids, *and* find time to visit my husband in rehab? A husband, I might add, who doesn't even remember me and our life together. That sounds easy."

"You can't do everything."

"I *need* to do everything. If I don't sell our house, how am I going to manage it all?"

"Your mother-in-law is here. Once the kids go back to school in the fall put them in after-school care, and let Elizabeth visit with Mark during the day while you work. You can spend the weekends with your family."

"You make it sound so easy, like I can pick right up where I left off. Who wants to hire a thirty-eight-year-old woman who's been out of the workplace for more than a decade?" When I made the choice to forgo a career and concentrate on raising my children, the possibility of losing Mark's income was a serious concern. Choosing the path of stay-at-home mom was a risk. It appeared I had chosen wrong.

"Shelby!" Jamie stood up and shouted at her daughter who had gone from a happy girl drawing with chalk to stamping her sandaled foot on Lana's artwork.

"Stop that. Be nice to Lana, she's your friend." Jamie looked back at me with a sigh. "Twelve years right?"

"Yes. I stopped working when Lana was born."

The blistering July sun poked its way free from a slow drifting cloud, making me sweat. I pulled my limp brown hair back into a bun. Drops of sweat slid down the back of my tank top and in between my breasts.

Jamie shook her head. "More than a decade of staying home and taking care of your children all day long. Maybe you should view getting a job as a vacation." She stared at me in an uncomfortable silence. "I don't know how you managed it all these years without going crazy. My job is my escape."

"That's one way to look at it, Miss Commercial Real Estate Appraiser. Aren't you always talking about how stressful your job is?"

"Yeah, but I thrive on the pressure. Plus making money gives me flexibility. If Michael fucks up, I don't need him."

And nannies raise your three young daughters. I looked over at Lana and Ben, two little people I knew better than anyone else in this world. I walked them to school each morning and got to know all of their friends. I visited my children's classrooms regularly to volunteer and formed close relationships with their teachers. Ben could show me what he was thinking with the slightest gesture. Lana shared her most important secrets with me during the long pauses on quiet days. Every choice we make as a parent means something else will be sacrificed.

I toyed with the hand-crafted hamsa on my delicate silver necklace. Jamie had it made for me by her favorite jeweler as a gift after the accident. The upside hand with two thumbs was supposed to ward off bad joojoo and keep me protected.

"After Lana was born, we took out a full million on Mark and a million on me, too. I figured, if he went first I would have enough to raise our daughter without ever having to worry about finances. If I went first, Mark could use the money to hire a live-in nanny, full time housekeeper, and an on call prostitute. Heck, with that type of setup, he would have it made."

"It does sound pretty sweet." Jamie elbowed me in the side, helping to lighten the mood.

"I wish I had been the one hurt in the accident. We all would have been better off."

Jamie stood again and yelled for Shelby to listen to Lana, then she pushed her sunglasses onto her head and sat back down. "Men always take the easier way out. Give them a choice between watching their kids or lying around wounded in a hospital bed, and they'll choose broken bones and brain injuries every day of the week."

"Jerks." I smiled for the first time in days.

"Seriously," Jamie continued, building up steam, "look at Mark's dad. Sure he flew out here and sat vigil at his son's bedside. But where is he now? He's back in Virginia, holding down the 'home front.' Meanwhile his wife is out here running herself ragged, looking after her son, driving her daughter-in-law nuts, and caring for her grandchildren. I ask you, who got the better deal?"

"Men," I laughed, despite my angst. "And we think we can't live without them."

"Bingo. Time to toughen up Natalie."

"What if can't?" I could hear the whine in my voice. "Couldn't I just crawl in a hole and play dead until this is all over?"

Jamie furrowed her brow, clearly frustrated. "You know, I'm going to be brutally honest. You have become so much weaker since you got married. It's like you threw in the towel on your own life and just gave it all over to Mark and the kids."

My mouth fell open, but I didn't utter a word.

"I mean it. You need to stop acting like a pussy."

How could she turn on me at my weakest moment? She might as well pluck out all my eyelashes in my sleep. "That was mean."

"Sorry, but I knew you before you were married with children. Remember how capable you were of tackling any challenge? You interned, worked at Jamba Juice part-time, and you still managed to get straight A's in college, all while planning a huge wedding.

Between you and Elizabeth, you'll handle this situation too." She put her hand on my knee as I resisted the urge to scowl at her.

"What about the fact that something is wrong with

Ben?" I asked. "His anxiety keeps getting worse. Pretty soon he is going to be carrying his green toothbrush in his pocket everywhere he goes. He needs me around."

"Did I tell you what I heard about the Baranovs?"

"The family on the other end of court?"

"Yeah, Gigi and David, and their daughter Piper."

"I know Piper is a bit off."

"More than a little. Apparently they've been leaving Piper with their housekeeper on Sundays while she cleaned their house. Gigi and David would go traipse off for Sunday breakfast, enjoy a little alone time and leave Piper to play with the housekeeper's two young daughters."

"What does this have to do with me?" I asked feeling a little annoyed with the change of subject.

"Listen. The maid, we'll call her Maria, stopped bringing her two daughters around, so Gigi asked Piper if she knew why. Turns out little seven-year-old Piper got a bucket one day and strung it up into a backyard tree with a rope. For fun she told Maria's two daughters who barely speak English, to strip naked and take turns swinging on the bucket while Piper played Miley Cyrus's video Wrecking Ball on her iPad."

"Are you making this up?"

"No. They did it too. The two girls, and then Piper, all took turns swinging naked on the bucket. And you know why Piper is on to her third private school now?"

"Marina told me. I wasn't sure if I believed her or not. She said Piper asked one the rabbi's daughters at her last school to stick a pencil up her vagina."

Jamie tapped the side of her sunglasses. "Exactly."

"Poor Gigi." I dropped my head to my knees at the thought of it. For a moment, Mark's year long stint in a physical rehabilitation center and Ben's toothbrush obsession didn't seem as terrible.

"There are always going to people who have it better than you, and there are always going to be women like Gigi, who have it even worse.

Mark will recover. Ben is quirky, but he is not over the top disturbed. I'll help out whenever I can, so will the other women in the neighborhood. You're not alone in all of this and you are not helpless. Time to put on your big girl panties and buck up."

I rolled my eyes at her in exasperation.

"You're like Dorothy with her ruby slippers," she said. "'You've always had the power my dear. You've had it all along,'" Jamie spoke in the sugared voice of Glinda from *The Wizard of Oz*.

"Gee, thanks lady, most powerful of all witches." I put my head on her shoulder to show her I loved her, even if she had called me a pussy who wears little girl underwear. "Should I start clicking my heels together now?"

"Forget the shoes. The magic's already inside you, Nat. That's the point."

Jabbing her gently in the ribs, I squinted into the sun. "You could be a little easier on me, you know."

"Yeah, but then I wouldn't be your best friend."

"I guess," I conceded, feeling a bit more strength emerging.

Tomorrow I would begin my search for a job. For the sake of my family, I would ignore the fear, and fatigue, and nagging suspicion that I was too old and too out of the loop to start a career or that my youngest child was too anxious for me to leave his side. I would tap in to my inner Dorothy. She was in there somewhere, she had to be.

SAMANTHA: WEDNESDAY, JULY 2

I scrubbed my kitchen's oversized, stainless steel sink in a fury of frantic strokes, searching my memories for missed clues.

When Cameron and I first began dating, he told me in great secrecy that his high school friends had voted him the Biggest Gossip. At the time, I didn't think anything of it. He also mentioned once that a handful of his ex-girlfriends had told him he was bad in bed, and he wanted to know if I thought that meant something.

If I was honest with myself, from the very beginning our sex life wasn't that great. He said he wanted to wait until he married me and after that it was steady, usually as often as three times a week, but it lacked passion.

One of our favorite past times before the kids came

along was spending the day at the mall. We would arrive early, shop until noon, grab lunch and then shop some more.

Still, half of my married friends—the ones that weren't complaining their husbands harassed them to give it up more often—swore to me their husband's were rarely interested in sex at all these days. Plenty of men liked to share the latest news with their friends, and lots of straight guys liked buying new clothes. These were not exactly giant red flags. Cameron covered his tracks well.

I turned off the faucet and slogged across our tiled floor to the living room. The couch got in my way, so I kicked it with full force. My bare toe throbbed in response, and I dropped down to assess the damage.

Sunlight streamed through our large open windows. I pulled back my hair and surveyed my beautiful home. The custom painted moss-green walls accentuated our numerous potted palms. My earth-toned granite countertops gleamed against an ornate tiled backsplash in the kitchen. We lived within walking distance of the ocean. I loved this house. I loved the life we had created here. I didn't want anything to change.

Massaging my injured toe, I noticed the floors. Ugly veins of filthy grout rampaged through our gorgeous tumbled travertine. Our tiles were perfect. The grout was an outright disgrace.

Cameron, who actually did have an academic

conference to attend in Portland, had stayed behind and wasn't due back for a couple more days. I fumed at the thought of him in that same hotel room. He could easily be hooking up with his student again. Why should I believe for one second that Cameron had truly sent him home? The thought fueled my need to do *something*, to scrub away all the imperfection from my life.

Gavin had about two hours or so left at his summer camp and both the girls were off with friends, leaving me plenty of time to clean. I pulled out a Costco-sized package of brand new toothbrushes and my favorite cleaning supply, Oxiclean.

With my free hand, I called my mother. She needed to know the truth.

"Mom?" I said when she picked up the phone. "How are you?" Kneeling down on the floor, I scrubbed a line of grout. Soapy brown particles floated in the tiny stream of water.

"I'm fine, just taking my lunch break a little late today." She took a long sucking drag from her cigarette. "What's going on with you?"

"Nothing."

"What are you up to?" she asked.

"Oh, I'm just scrubbing the floors. You should see how much better the little section I'm working on looks." I grabbed a sponge and wiped up the moisture on the floor. The color beneath flaunted a creamy beige.

Mom exhaled, and I could picture her standing outside the Klamath Falls Diner on the blacktopped parking lot. "What's wrong?"

"It's Cameron." I raked the toothbrush across a deep layer of filth, trying to push away the pain in my voice. "I caught him with another man."

"What do you mean?"

"I mean he was messing around with a man. He's gay, Mom. He likes guys. He fucked some former student of his last night in a hotel room in Portland, Oregon. When I walked in on them, his boyfriend called me ma'am."

My mother gasped.

I evaluated the floor as I waited for her to speak. The scrubbed lines sparkled next to the tile and made a mockery of the rest of the grout. If I could work on a few more sections, it would look so much better.

"Wait a second, let's back up here. Tell me exactly what's going on."

I put her on speaker-phone and worked the floor on my hands and knees while I recounted the whole story. Every sordid detail. "The thing is," I stood up and began pacing, "I don't think I can let him go. I like the life we have together. Is that crazy?"

"Oh, honey. Of course you still love him. A woman's heart doesn't turn off that easy."

"No, I mean is it crazy that I want to *keep* my husband? That even though I know he's fucking other men, I want him to stay with me?"

"I don't know. I think Cameron messed up big time. Cheating is cheating, whether it's with a man or a woman. Personally, I'd like to kick his butt right about now." She sighed into the phone, and I could picture her shaking her head. "But to answer your question, no, I don't think you have anything to feel bad about. You've been married for nearly two decades, your feelings are not something that can be manipulated at will. Change is hard for anybody."

"What if I asked him to stay? What if he could see his boyfriends quietly on the side and we just didn't talk about it?"

"Is that really what you want?"

I ignored her question. "It would make his parents happy, and the kids, and maybe him too. He seems to like the whole domestic thing." I swiped at the renegade tears freefalling down my cheeks.

Growing up in Klamath Falls, I didn't get invited over to my friends' houses as often as the other girls. The well respected married men and women in town looked at my mother and me like we were savages. Our lives went from fairy tale to tragic when Dad moved out.

My mom never even dated after Dad took off. All she had was me, her nine-to-five waitressing job, and her best friend Elena, a married woman without a child of her own.

"But what about you? Who cares what Cameron wants?"

I got back on the floor and resumed scrubbing. "Honestly, Cameron and I have a really good life. Why throw it all away? Eventually, I could find someone to hook up with on the side too. I've heard there are a lot of couples like that around here. Wealthy gay men and their beautiful beards, they even have swinger parties. Modern day family."

"That sounds good to you?" She coughed and then cleared her throat. "I know I may have not been the best role model for you as a single mom, but that doesn't mean your life is going to turn out the same as mine. I chose not to date after your father left. You could have someone who appreciates you in a heartbeat if that's what you want."

I pictured her stubbing out her cigarette on the edge of the sidewalk, checking the time on her phone. She should have been back on the clock at least thirty minutes ago.

"Why break up our family, though? Nothing has really changed. The only difference is now I know the reality of the situation. No one else would have to know the truth."

"This isn't about what other people think."

"I was just talking out loud. Everything is coming at me all at once." I paused to survey my work. My black yoga pants may have been soaked in soapy detergent and the pink, green, blue, and yellow, frazzled toothbrushes lay thrashed and useless, but my floor looked immaculate. "I don't know what I want Mom. I'm just so angry and feel like such a loser right now.

Listen, I gotta go. It's time to pick up Gavin from camp. Love you."

NATALIE: TUESDAY, JULY 15

Only one week after Mark moved into the physical rehab center, I found myself standing in the KLAW-TV parking lot in West Hollywood, moments away from my first official job interview in more than a decade.

This had been Jamie's idea. She was the one who watched the show and heard their request. Just a single day after her pep-talk, she was the one who called me and told me I needed to give it a try. I had interned at San Diego's KPAL Channel 4 News during college and had been an assignment editor until Lana was born. Working as a television reporter had been a fantasy of mine—a dream I had supposedly set aside for the sake of my children. If I was completely honest with myself, I had also been afraid of failure. Babies were a great reason to stay home.

Now, however, *Good Morning LA,* the nationally syndicated news program taped out of Los Angeles, was looking for a stay-at-home mom to join their small cast of commentators. The chosen candidate would work on Mondays, Wednesdays and Fridays. She would add a new perspective to the group and represent the mommy viewers at home. It was a simultaneously terrifying and electrifying opportunity.

Within days an old producer buddy had arranged for me to record a proper resume tape and one of his editors jazzed it up. So here I was, in one big whirlwind, dressed in a brand new tailored gray suit with a bright pink silk blouse, ready for business. More than twelve years after I resigned, I was walking back onto familiar ground, only this time, in a much bigger city.

Hearing back from *Good Morning LA* was like falling into a time machine and being given a do-over. They liked my tape and invited me to the studio for a mock show performance. This was a chance to not only get back into a newsroom, but to serve as one of the actual anchors.

My head throbbed. I didn't just desperately want this, I had come to believe I needed it. Sweeping aside the voices of self doubt, I tried to ignore the shivers of nervousness and unabashed excitement. I was here to support my family. I would hold it together for the good of everyone.

***

"So you know Dan, the photog who eye-fucks all the interns?" Two women in their early thirties sat cross legged on the concrete steps smoking cigarettes and exchanging newsroom gossip. "I heard he left his wife for some nineteen-year-old chick who serves lattes at Starbucks."

The other woman took a drag and blew out the smoke. "What a loser."

"Totally," her co-worker agreed, her shiny forehead perspiring under the harsh sun.

Glass doors loomed behind them, mirroring their slim reflections.

"Morning," I waved as I pushed passed them. They tilted their heads and looked at me with a cool gleam of curiosity and practiced apathy.

Another world waited for me inside. Under the glow of florescent lights, the newsroom had a magnetic energy. It was a living, breathing animal all its own. Reporters, producers, assistant producers, and assistant assignment editors rushed around the main floor as if there was an emergency evacuation taking place and they needed to grab their most precious belongings. Phones rang, faxes beeped, reporters sat in front of little television screens, fast forwarding and rewinding video while they peered into the monitors and took fastidious notes.

It was organized chaos at its finest. This place felt familiar, almost comfortable. Back in my younger days,

I fed off the intensity of a bustling newsroom and all the quirky people who worked there. Another rush of adrenaline pulsed through me.

"Natalie? Over here." A tall, attractive women dressed in a short skirt and dangerously high heels waved me toward the reception desk.

"Kim?"

"Yes, come on over." She motioned me toward a slim blonde receptionist with a bright smile. "Brenda here has your badge. Everyone is ready for you."

I inhaled a large gulp of air and accepted my nametag. "Should I go freshen up before we get started?"

"No, we have someone to do that for you. I'll walk you over to the makeup room. Once Louisa's touched up your hair and face, I'll come back and get you set up in the studio." Kim handed me a stack of tissue thin pink papers as we walked. "These are your scripts. You would normally get these in the morning and go over them during prep. Take a look through the stories now so you'll be ready to go."

My stomach danced into knots. This wasn't going to work out. I'd do my thing and then drive back home to my real life. Until I found a sensible job, I had other more practical options for paying the bills. Like dipping into our 401K. "It's just for fun," I murmured under my breath.

"Did you say something?" Kim tipped her pretty head to the side and smiled at me.

"Just giving myself a little pep talk."

"Good. Don't worry about a thing. This is all entertainment. If you have a good time, so will your audience. Try to relax. Okay? Here we are." She gestured her hand like Vanna White. "This is the makeup room. I'll see you in a few." With that she darted off, leaving me on my own.

Before I could decide what to do next, a curvy woman with thick black hair and heavy makeup breezed past me and into the brightly lit room. She looked a lot like my mother-in-law did in her fifties. "Hey, I'm Louisa. Come on over here and take a seat."

I did as she said, sitting down in a big black swivel chair placed in front of a mirror that covered the length of the room. Large naked light bulbs shone above, highlighting my every flaw. Tiny lines zigzagged across my forehead and crept across the edges of my eyes. "Ugh, I hope you have some magic tricks up your sleeve. I'm looking far too old and tired for a close up."

She picked up a large poufy makeup brush and dusted it in blush. "Sweetie, I've been doing this for thirty years. I guarantee you by the time I'm finished, you'll look as gorgeous as an underage fashion model. You've got good bones. I'm just gonna do some cover up work so you don't look like an oily ghost on camera."

"What more could a girl ask for?" I laughed as I settled in and reviewed my scripts.

After shellacking my face, Louisa picked up a

comb and a flat iron, working on my hair. Once it was smoothed out she sprayed in volumizer and rubbed it in like shampoo. From the corner of my eye, I could see her pursing her lips in thought. "Is everything ok?"

"You know," Louisa lowered her voice and kicked the door shut. "I shouldn't say anything, but I overhear everything in this newsroom."

I set my scripts on my lap, feeling my stomach tighten again with anxiety. She made eye contact with me in the mirror. "The producers are saying you're the one. They absolutely loved your tape. You are the last candidate in here and the other ladies didn't make the cut. They were either too stiff or too desperate."

I broke into a light sweat. "You're kidding me."

"Nope, not at all. They're looking for, you know, someone the ladies at home can relate to. If it's not you, they're gonna go through a whole 'nother round of moms."

"Are you sure they meant me? Natalie Delisse?" Every piece of me hoped she was right. This job would be a life changer.

"Sweetie, I'm positive. They love your whole wholesome San Diego mama thing with your sick hubbie. Viewers will eat you up."

Before I had time to let the news fully settle in, Kim popped her head back inside the room to fetch me. "You all set?" she asked, flashing me her full set of chewing gum commercial teeth.

I wrapped a tendril of my newly quaffed hair

around my finger. Louisa had puffed up the top and lacquered it in generous poofs of Aqua Net before running her flat iron over the rest. She had transformed my ordinary brunette locks into a silky polished masterpiece, worthy of a Miss America pageant. "I'm as ready as I'll ever be," I said to Kim.

"You look phenomenal."

"Thanks."

Louisa looked over at Kim. "Just give me a few more minutes. I'm almost finished."

She spun me away from the mirror as Kim stood waiting and whipped out a few more brushes, some small, some big enough to paint on wall-to-wall canvas. I felt her darkening my eyeliner, adding shadow, and gluing on false lashes. She contoured the sides of my cheeks and applied a brighter lipstick. With a big smile, she whirled me back around in my chair.

I looked in the mirror and saw myself transformed. It was me, only in Technicolor. My brown eyes popped and sparkled. My cheek bones appeared higher, and the lines tracking my forehead had disappeared. I looked like the confident, sexy women you see on Fox evening news. I was glamorous, flawless, fearless. "Wow, Louisa." I beamed at her in the mirror.

"You've been Louisa-fied."

"I love it." I touched at my hair and admired my reflection in the mirror. I was going into battle, and this was my war paint.

Slipping out of the makeup chair, I held tight to my

scripts. "Ready."

"Great. Follow me." Kim led me to the set just a few feet away. Three overstuffed chairs gathered near a long coffee table on a small concrete soundstage. Two familiar faces occupied the chairs, their hair shining under a halo of hot spotlights. Primping and posturing in their cozy living room set, the two hosts acted as if they were preparing to run lines in a serious college production rather than deliver morning news and light entertainment. I fought to contain the nervous quivering in my hands and legs, to remind myself of my new warrior status.

The main anchor woman, a gorgeous leggy blonde dressed in a slinky yellow skirt suit, studied her notes without looking up to acknowledge me. Her partner stood to shake my hand.

"Jack Dillon, it's nice to meet you. We've heard good things about you." He pumped my hand up and down and motioned to his co-host. "This is Dana. Dana Aldridge. She's not very talkative before the camera starts rolling." Jack chuckled, charming me with his movie star smile. Dana ignored me and continued to study her notes. I imagined her bald and toothless, it made me happy.

I did like Jack. He was a man women would describe as aging with character. His classic Hollywood, well kempt salt and pepper hair and slightly weathered skin suited him.

"Great, now that we all know each other," Kim

waved her hand for me to sit in the remaining third chair. "We'll go ahead and get you set up. Here." She handed me a small ear piece that resembled a hearing aid. "Place this in your ear. It's so the director can talk to you and give you instructions while you're on air. He'll tell you when to talk and when to wrap things up. He will also give you instructions for which camera to look at, by either saying camera one, two, or three. See how there's a numbered sign above each of the cameras?" I nodded, taking a closer look. The large, automated cameras were mounted on intricate pedestals the size of burly, overgrown men.

"Great." Kim handed me a little black microphone the size of a small thimble. It was attached to a skinny, flexible cord. "I'm going to lace this up your top and clip it to the edge of your blouse."

"I know how to do it," I assured her, taking the microphone and putting it in place. "I wore one when I made my audition tape. Plus, I watched the anchors at my old San Diego station clip theirs on every night." I wanted to remind her I wasn't completely new to this business. I wasn't starting from scratch.

"Excellent." She reached out and straightened my microphone. "Then you're also familiar with a mic check. When the director asks for one, go ahead and talk so he can make sure your sound levels are set correctly." Kim nodded as I spoke out loud. "One, two, three. One, two, three. Check. Check. Check."

"Okay, great job. Why don't we give this a run-through before we begin rolling."

Camera One moved backward like a life sized robot and turned at a right angle to capture Dana, Jack, and me smiling into its cold black lens.

The director's voice spoke into my ear. "Natalie, I want you to start off looking at Camera Two. Once Jack and Dana say hello and introduce you, turn to Camera One to talk. Got it?"

"Yes." I straightened the stack of scripts resting on my lap. *Have fun and the audience will have fun,* I repeated Kim's advice in my head. I could do this. I just needed to be myself, not that I was entirely sure of who that was anymore.

NATALIE: FRIDAY, AUGUST 15

Elizabeth and I loaded Lana and Ben into the car in near silence. The kids hadn't seen their dad since he left the hospital a little over a month ago. "Are you guys excited?" I asked as Lana buckled herself in.

Things hadn't gone well during their first couple of visits to the ICU. At first the machines and tubes attached to their unconscious father terrified them. Then, when Mark came out of his coma, it scared Lana and Ben that Mark didn't recognize them and that he didn't seem very interested in getting to know them either. So I made the difficult decision to cut off further visits until he was more lucid and better able to interact with our kids.

"Ok, Ben, I brought a juice box and some graham crackers to eat on the drive over. You sure you don't have to pee?"

"He just went," Elizabeth answered for him.

Elizabeth had her own concerns about this trip. She'd spent the last few days talking to Mark's therapists and me about how seeing the kids again could affect Mark. She feared a setback. I was more worried about how the visit would affect Lana and Ben.

"You kiddos all ready to go?" I asked, sliding into the driver's side and putting the key in the ignition.

"Yeah," they mumbled one after the other.

Elizabeth turned back from the passenger seat to look at Ben. "Make sure you don't get crumbs all over your booster seat."

None of us responded.

When I first told the kids about the car accident, Lana broke down in quiet tears while Ben became hysterical—snot flowing, spit flying. He asked if I was going to die next, if I would leave him without a mommy or daddy. Lana did her best to assure her brother she would take care of him herself if anything bad happened to me.

As we pulled out of Kingston Court's tranquil streets and headed toward Mark's rehab center, Ben banged his head rhythmically against the back of his booster seat and sang a song he had made up. Lana sent text messages and played games on her phone.

"Daddy is really looking forward to seeing you two. He told me on my last visit," I said, checking for their reaction in the rearview mirror. Our nervous energy could fuel an entire town. "How are you feeling right now?"

"Scared," Ben said.

Soon after his first visit to see Mark in the hospital, Ben refused to get out of the car when I dropped him off at pre-school. I would carry him against his will to his classroom and then listen to my boy scream for me as I walked away. I eventually relented and pulled him out before summer vacation. It didn't help. At bedtime, I found bite marks on his arms and, as the weeks passed, I watched his chewed up cuticles grow red and puffy from infection.

Lana set her phone on her lap and held Ben's hand. "It's okay Benjie. I'm here for you and so is Mommy." She smiled at him with her deep dimpled cheeks. With her pixie haircut and big blue eyes, she couldn't have looked any sweeter.

I took pride in my daughter's compassion, knowing she was struggling, too. "Ben, Daddy is fully awake now, and he's looking forward to giving you and your sister a big hug."

"You have to be extra careful with your father." Elizabeth cut in. "It's important to remember he is still tired and he can't visit for too long."

I clutched the steering wheel tighter, willing her to shut her mouth. Couldn't she see the dark circles rimming Ben's baby blue eyes? Didn't she notice Lana had lost weight in the past month, leaving her petite frame even tinier. Her homework was also becoming less of a priority. I worried she was losing her childhood. Mark could rest when we left. It was his children who needed our support today. We needed to make this good for them.

"Ben has nothing to worry about. We're just going to say hello and give Dad some hugs and kisses." I changed lanes and looked back into the rearview mirror. "He misses you both very much and your visit today means the world to him."

Lana gave a half-hearted smile and picked up her cell phone, keeping her eyes averted from mine.

"Mama?" Ben asked as he continued to bang his head, his puffs of curly blond hair swaying in motion. "Why can't Daddy just come home with us? Hasn't he been there long enough?"

"It sure feels like it doesn't it?" I reached my hand around the back of my seat and squeezed the bottom of his foot. The doctor had increased Ben's anti-anxiety medication, but it didn't seem to make much of a difference.

"Honey, can you please stop that banging. You're giving Grandma a headache," Elizabeth asked Ben as she puckered her mouth and applied a thick layer of brick-red lipstick. The aging Southern beauty queen had to look her best for the rehab staff.

"He can't," Lana replied. "He does it when he needs to calm himself."

"That's right Lana. You're fine, Ben," I reassured my son. "Daddy's going to have to stay at this new place a little while longer. Remember how I told you he bumped his head and now he has to relearn a bunch of stuff? They need to teach Daddy to use a fork and knife like a big guy. He has to get strong again and learn how to tie his shoes and write things down on paper. Important stuff like you learned at preschool."

"But why can't he come home after school like I did? I can teach him those things."

A car pulled in front of us and I hit the brakes, flashbacks of the accident making my underarms prickle and sweat. The sound of metal smashing reverberated in my skull. "Ben, Daddy needs to learn it all at once, very quickly. He wants to figure everything out right away so he can come home and take care of you and your sister and Mommy again."

"I know." He kicked the back of my seat. "You said that."

***

Walking into rehab felt like visiting an upscale prison. It looked okay, but I was certain none of its residents or visitors wanted to be here. The cheerful pictures on the walls and colorful fish aquarium didn't fool anyone.

When we made our way into his room, Mark searched Ben's face. "Hi?"

"Hi." Ben clamped on to my left leg while I pulled up a metal chair and took a seat.

"Lana?" Mark looked at his daughter. When I saw Mark earlier in the week, I had prompted him on what to say during this visit. So far, he was following directions.

Lana scanned her cell phone, letting the bangs of her short brown hair fall across her eyes.

"Hey." Lana replied to her father as if he were a curious stranger. "We made you some pictures." She handed him her detailed drawing of a colorful butterfly and a picture Ben had drawn with crayons of action stick figures.

"Daddy," Ben said. "I don't like it here."

"Sure thing," Mark said back. He still wasn't much for conversation these days.

"What happened to your hair" Ben asked Mark.

"Bug," I answered for Mark, "remember I told you they had to shave it? I think daddy's buzz cut makes him look tough."

"Well I sure like it," Elizabeth said, taking a seat facing Mark. "I'm glad he decided to keep his hair this way. It suits him." She looked over at my son sitting on the floor, his arms still wrapped around my leg. "Ben, why don't you tell your father about your day?"

"I just hung out with Gabby girl."

"Your kitty cat?" she prodded.

"Yeah, we have such interesting conversations. We meow and meow about how much meow we have."

I giggled at Ben's remark as Elizabeth sat back in her chair rubbing her fingers into her temple.

"You and your kitty are such good friends." I kissed the top of Ben's tow head.

Mark didn't react. The blank look on his face resembled the poker face expressions my grandmother made before she passed away from complications due to Alzheimer's.

"So," I said to Mark. "Lana just finished reading a new book she really liked."

He looked at his daughter with interest. "What book?"

Lana shrugged her shoulders. "I don't remember."

"Come on sweetie," I nudged her. "You know which one I'm talking about." Ben let go of my leg and climbed onto my lap. "It's the story about the all girls school that teaches them how to be spies."

Lana, twisted a lock of dark brown hair and looked at the ceiling. "Oh yeah. It's called *I'd Tell You I Love You, But Then I'd Have To Kill You.*"

Elizabeth, Mark, and I all nodded our heads in a cold wave of silence. The air conditioner rattled on, making it even chillier. Ben slid back down my lap and shoved his head up my long lavender skirt.

"Benjamin," Elizabeth snapped. "Get out of your mother's dress."

"Noooo." He clamped his arms around both my legs, his body disappearing completely under the protection of the soft fabric. "I want to go home."

The sixteen-year-old girl knocking around inside my bones wanted to bolt down the hallway. This meeting was not going well.

Elizabeth tugged on the sleeves of her blue collared blouse as I searched my brain for any excuse to leave. We could try this again next week, over time the kids would get used to these visits. "Okay. Well, I think we should probably get going. I need to give the kids lunch and Mark, it looks like you could use some rest hon."

He gave me a closed lip smile, his true feelings unreadable. "Thank you for visiting guys. It's always so nice to see you. Ben, Lana, you are wonderful kids. I'm so grateful I got to spend time with you today."

Ben stayed hidden up my skirt while Lana did her best to ignore every adult in the room.

"Guys," I prompted, "Want to say goodbye to Daddy? Give him a hug? He was really hoping for a hug."

My daughter slumped off her chair as if she were exiting a slide. "Bye Dad." She gave him a quick squeeze before moving toward me and looking at her little brother's feet. "Benjie, come on out and hold my hand. We're leaving now."

I pulled my skirt off of Ben's body making an effort not to flash my husband. "Ben? Want to say goodbye?"

Ben looked over at Mark as he took his sister's hand. Squishing his face against her ribcage, he offered Mark a muffled goodbye.

I gave Mark a smile and rubbed the side of Ben's head. "You guys can give your dad a hug on our next visit. It'll give you both something to look forward to."

As the three of us walked to the door with Elizabeth gathering her things and trailing behind us, Lana looked back at Mark. "Bye daddy. We miss you." She pinched up her face the way she did when she was fighting tears and walked straight out of the room, tugging Ben behind her.

SAMANTHA: LABOR DAY WEEKEND (AUGUST 30TH – SEPTEMBER 1ST)

Before Cameron and I had a chance to plan out our next steps as a family, our oldest daughter Sophia took off in the middle of the night. We woke in the morning to a note saying she had gone out and that we shouldn't worry, she'd be in touch with us soon.

When she finally called several hours later, she was sobbing and apologetic. She told us she was near my hometown in Klamath Falls, Oregon. Sophia had already crossed the state line. Some boy she met on her visit to my mom's place over summer vacation had stolen down to San Diego to pick her up and drive her there.

After a whole lot of handwringing and argument, we all agreed she would finish the drive North and stay the night with her Grandma Marla. Cameron would leave immediately to fetch her while I stayed home with Savanna and Gavin.

The following morning, as I awaited their return, I went back to scrubbing the floor tiles like they were covered in black tar, going over each one with a diamond cutter's precision. If I could just focus on what I could control, the rest of my life would fall into place.

I had taken our dog on a quick walk earlier and overhead Marina the Gossip chattering to Beth the Spazz. Word of Sophia's disappearing act had already spread like a bad virus. Marina told Beth it was my fault Sophia left.

"She's jealous of her daughter. It's no wonder Sophia ran away. Samantha always insults her and acts like they're in some sort of competition for Cameron's attention. It's so sad."

I couldn't shake the hissing sound of Marina's whispered words. What did *she* know.

Truth be told, she was probably jealous of *me*. Marina, with her kinky blonde hair and sagging face. She had lost and gained and lost again, at least thirty pounds since she moved to Kingston Court five years ago, and her husband was constantly checking me out and offering me free bottles of wine from the chain of discount liquor stores he owned. Not to mention, I knew one of her sons had a recent run in with law for selling pot and prescription pills to his high school buddies. She *wished* she had it as good as me.

When my cell phone rang, I set down the toothbrush and slid my finger across the answer screen.

"Hey, it's Cameron. We're getting ready to pull off the freeway. We should be there in about ten to fifteen minutes."

"How is she?" I asked.

"She's nervous. She's worried about how you'll react. We talked a lot on the ride home."

"Did she tell you what happened exactly?" I asked, sensing he was holding out on me.

Cameron breathed into the phone. "Just what I told you already. As soon as she crossed the California border, Sophia realized what a big mistake she made and asked the boy... what's his name Sophia?" I heard my daughter's voice in the background. "Trevor. Yeah, she asked Trevor to drop her off at your mom's."

I gripped the phone tighter than necessary. "Do you think she already knows about your affair?" I figured that was the real reason she took off. She must have sensed Cameron was cheating and lying to us all.

"No, Sam, nothing like that."

I didn't believe him. "Okay, well, I'll let you concentrate on the road. Jess is watching Gavin and Savanna for me, so we can all talk when you get here."

"See you in a few minutes." Cameron clicked off the phone.

I began to pace. Up and down the hallway, back and forth, past the picture window showcasing the Jacaranda tree, its branches barren after shedding vibrant violet-blue flowers earlier in the season. I threw my hair up in a French twist, then took it down again. Why was Sophia nervous about my reaction? Shouldn't a girl who just ran away with a boy be more worried about her father? Feeling claustrophobic in my grimy yoga pants, I ran up the stairs and changed clothes.

Cameron's car alarm beeped. Our little ten pound Jack Russell barked and began dancing on her hind legs as Cameron and Sophia walked through the door. My daughter hid behind her long blonde hair, setting down her bags and scooping up the squiggling, squealing dog. "Hey Darby. How are you baby girl? Did you miss me dog friend?" Darby screeched with glee and broke free of Sophia's grasp. She landed on all fours and shot out of the room. Two seconds later she raced back toward Sophia, her nails clacking and digging for traction against the slick gleaming tiles I'd just scrubbed clean.

I stood in front of my daughter, moving aside the dog. "Sophia, am *I* going to get a hug?"

She hung her head lower, her hair covering her blue eyes, and walked into my open arms.

"I was so worried." Tears slipped down my cheeks. "What if something terrible happened to you?"

"I know," her voice cracked. "I was scared, too. It was stupid."

I hugged her tighter, inhaling the familiar scent of her favorite vanilla-jasmine body lotion. "Why Sophia? What were you thinking?"

"I don't know. Trevor called me about a few days

ago and thought it would be fun to hang out over Labor Day Weekend. It was his idea. I said no at first, but then I thought, why not?"

"How about because you would scare the life out of your mother and father? Because it wasn't safe? God knows what could have happened to you."

"I knew it would piss you off. I guess that's part of the reason, too."

The hairs on my arms stood stiff. "What?" I asked, trying to ignore those aggravating neighbor women's voices rattling in my head.

"I don't know. But, I can't always be perfect. I'm not you."

I released my grip on her. There was no way this could be my fault. I was a good mother. "What are you talking about?"

Sophia scowled in Cameron's direction. "I told you she wouldn't understand."

"Understand what?" I glared at my traitor husband, feeling thrown off balance once again. "Were you talking about me on the drive down? Did you let her think this was all okay, just some teenage rebellion against her cruel and unreasonable mother?" Cameron shook his head in response. "Absolutely not. She knows she's the one responsible for her poor choices. I took away her—"

"What did she mean when she said I wouldn't understand?" Crossing my arms across my chest, I looked back to Sophia. I had dedicated the last sixteen years of my life to my daughter. Why was she turning on me? "Sophia? Answer the question."

She ignored me, walking over to the staircase and collapsing onto the stairs with a level of drama only a teenage girl could muster. I watched her plant her face atop her crossed arms.

"Sophia?"

"What?" She raised her head, her eyes shrouded in her thick mane of hair.

"What wouldn't I understand?"

She wiped wet tears onto the limp sleeve of her oversized sweatshirt. "That I'm tired of you treating me like I'm your project. Like you know best about everything."

My head jerked back in hurt and surprise. "What are you talking about? I don't do anything more than give you good advice."

"Advice on how to be just like you."

"Who would you rather be like? The Klamath Falls boy you ran away with? A boy who will probably be lucky to graduate high school. Is that a better role model for you?"

"No," she wailed, losing all of her self-control. "I just want to be myself."

"I'm the adult." I fought to restrain the sharp edge in my voice. My daughter and husband were ganging up on me, and I didn't deserve it. "It's my job to guide you."

"It's not your job to dictate my every move. I'm

not two years old anymore."

"Really? You're balled up on the floor crying and throwing a temper tantrum because you ran away from your mommy. Sounds like two-year-old behavior to me."

Sophia pushed all the hair out of her face and looked directly at me. Her gorgeous eyes, cold and uncaring. "I really hate you right now."

"Samantha," Cameron stepped inside my personal space and put his hand on my arm as if to stop me from lunging at our daughter. "Let's not make this worse. Sophia is sorry. She knows she made a mistake. She also has some concerns about her relationship with you that may or may not be valid."

I scowled at Cameron, wishing he would dissolve into a puddle of nothingness. "So this is all about me? You're on her side and this is all *my* fault?"

He let his hand fall off my arm. "Of course not. I'm not on anybody's side. There are no sides. We're a family." He paused and looked over at Sophia. "I think it'd be best if the two of you sat down with a therapist in a neutral environment and discussed this."

The heat pulsating through my chest and arms was going to boil me alive. I could not believe we were having this conversation. Why wasn't Cameron standing up for me? Why wasn't *he* the bad guy in all of this? He was the liar and the cheater. He was the one putting our family in jeopardy. "Our sixteen-year-old daughter runs away from home, and you want *me* to see a shrink?"

"Sophia feels disconnected from you, and I know for a fact that your children are more important to you than anything in this world. Sometimes talking to a neutral third party can help." He looked back at our daughter who lay curled up in the fetal position like a dead martyr. Darby licked at her face and nuzzled her neck. "This isn't the end of the world. Sophia made a very poor choice and she's going to suffer the consequences. She already knows she is grounded for the next month. No driving, no phone, and no computers unless it's for school work."

Sophia lifted her head from the stairs. "Can I go to my room?"

"Go." I rubbed at the new tears welling in my eyes.

Sophia kept her face turned away from me as she took the steps in slow motion, moving as if she were filled with wet sand. Darby trailed behind her, like my daughter needed protection. I watched them both climb the carpeted stairs and disappear into the hallway.

Old hurts clawed beneath the surface, thrashing to act out. I remembered a quote from my favorite college professor, Dr. Romeo, *That which cannot be rationalized must be expressed.* I couldn't handle much more rejection.

"Thanks a lot Cameron. You totally fuck us over and now I'm the bad guy? You're making me look like the asshole? Thanks for absolutely nothing."

NATALIE: MONDAY, SEPTEMBER 1

Drivers laid heavy on their horns. Travelers rushed by on foot in every direction, each one looking more glamorous than the next. The women carried designer hand bags and dragged sleek luggage on wheels. Six weeks after my first interview, I was standing curbside at LAX waiting for a woman named Inna Kozlova. They told me she was Russian, originally from Moscow, and that her name was pronounced Ee-na.

The busty blonde standing beside me dropped her bottle of red wine, letting out a yelp as it crashed against the concrete. I had landed the coveted national television show gig and this was my christening.

Guilt seeped through my veins. I didn't have the right to feel excited. I should be missing my family. It wasn't appropriate to be soaking in the sights and sounds of a big city and buzzing with anticipation. I checked the screen on my cell phone for any messages and looked for my ride.

That's when I spotted a small, well manicured hand waving up from the driver's side of a black Escalade. "Hey, Natalie," she said in a gravely, Demi Moore sounding voice.

I rolled my small suitcase toward the massive vehicle and took a quick look through the passenger window. A stunning young woman with big brown eyes and full rose colored lips smiled and popped open the rear hatch. "Throw your stuff in the back and let's get out of here." The bumper sticker on her Escalade read *I don't believe the LIBERAL media.*

Horns blasted. An airport security officer motioned cars forward as I hoisted my carry-on into her vehicle. Inside the SUV, Inna squeezed the side of my arm by way of introduction. "Listen," she spoke with only the slightest hint of a Russian accent. "Buckle up. The people in this city drive like animals."

"Great." I clicked on my belt. Ever since the accident, traffic made me nervous.

"Don't worry," Inna tried to reassure me. "I'll take any of these motherfuckers down if they get in our way."

I nodded, refusing to show fear or excitement.

"You like Rita Ora?"

I shook my head. "Never heard of her. Are we going to be interviewing her?"

Inna lit up a cigarette and laughed, tossing her dark blonde hair to the side. "I wish. No, she's a singer. I'll play my favorite song for you." She pushed several buttons before a strong clear voice came blasting out of the surround-sound speakers. It was all about an aggressive woman telling a guy that she had decided to sleep with him, so he better get rid of his girlfriend.

Inna mouthed the words to every lyric. She had the entire song memorized. I envisioned Inna in an edgy studio apartment somewhere in West Hollywood, crawling across a concrete floor and demanding some innocent young man come over and please her.

"What do you think?" she shouted over the music.

"It's fun. I like it." I bounced my knee to the beat, feeling the bass reverberate in my bones. Between the energy of this city, a high profile new job, and the intense girl behind the wheel of her massive SUV, it was hard to keep calm.

Good Morning LA had sent me a first class round-trip ticket to fly from San Diego to Los Angeles and back. Inna, a production assistant on the show, offered to pick me up and let me stay the night at her place. My first choice would have been a limo ride from San Diego and a hotel room, but the powers that be wanted me well rested the night before my first show, and they seemed to think this was the way to go. I was not at all sure they made the right decision.

When the song ended, Inna turned down the volume. "So what do you think of LA?"

"So far so good."

"Cool," she took another drag of her cigarette and veered into the next lane, flipping off the driver beside her as she sped along the 405. "I told you these motherfuckers were animals. Do you want to go back to my place and get settled, or would you rather grab some drinks first? Whatever you want is fine with me."

I gripped the door handle. "I'd like to get to bed early tonight. You know, before my big first day."

"No problem. My kids are asleep, so when we get there, you have to be quiet. Okay?"

"You have children?" I asked, trying to imagine this woman as a mother. "You look so young."

She smiled and gave herself a quick glance in the rearview mirror. "Twenty-eight. I'm practically elderly as far as men in this town go. I might as well dig my grave and bury myself in it."

"What does that make me, a walking corpse?"

"You're fine," she assured me in her deep throaty voice. "You look fantastic. We're just not fresh meat anymore. You know?"

I noted the large rock on her ring finger. "Good thing we're not looking, huh?"

"Speak for yourself. My husband moved into an apartment a couple of months ago. I haven't been laid in over a year."

"It's been a while for me too," I admitted. "My husband is living in a physical rehabilitation center. He barely remembers who I am, let alone shows any desire to touch me."

Inna put her hair up in a clip as she drove, the car veering slightly to the left. "I heard about the accident. Were you two close?" She switched lanes for the umpteenth time, making my heart beat in fast forward.

"We are. He's the best husband and father I could ask for. It's just hard to feel connected to him right now with everything going on. But I love him dearly."

"That's so romantic." She white knuckled the steering wheel. "My husband's a piece of shit. I wish *he* would get in a car accident."

I felt my eyes widen in surprise as we exited the 405 North and headed east on Wilshire Boulevard. Inna was so over the top, just like this crazy overpopulated town. I'd spent most of my life avoiding Los Angeles and its notorious traffic jams. Sitting here now, I couldn't decide if I was more terrified or electrified by it all. My toes, my fingers, all of my limbs, were buzzing.

"I live here in Westwood. You'll like my place. It's nice and quiet when the kids are sleeping."

"Who's watching them?" I rolled the window down halfway and let the warm night air blow across my face. It didn't smell anything like San Diego, more like a mixture of gasoline and something else unsavory, like week-old egg salad. I rolled my window back up.

Inna didn't seem to notice anything amiss. "My mom is watching my kids. Don't worry, she'll take off as soon as we get there. No need to make small talk.

Just say hello and I'll walk you to your room."

She pulled her car to an abrupt stop on an upward sloped driveway and shut off the engine. Her well lit house looked big and modern with clean wood lines. A mature Japanese Maple tree stood tall in her front yard. We hopped down out of our seats and after grabbing my luggage, made our way up to the gated entryway.

The inside of her home was immaculate, a contemporary space with honeyed wood floors and designer furniture. Inna had set up her formal living room as a well organized playroom, complete with colorful rubber mats and bins full of Barbie dolls and fire trucks. It was nothing like I expected.

"Privet mama. Eto tah devochka s novostey pro kotoruyu ya tebe govorila. Ne razgovarivay, razbudish detey." Inna spoke to her mom who laid half asleep on the couch.

I mouthed a hello while Inna shepherded me to the downstairs guest room. "Make yourself at home. The bathroom is right across the hall and the refrigerator and cupboards are fully stocked." Inna flicked on the light and closed the door.

I set down my bags and looked around the softly lit bedroom. The serenity of this space, with its cream walls and luxurious queen-sized bed, stood in screaming contrast from the rushed madness outside.

Would my first day at work feel as chaotic as my drive here from the airport? What if I sat down in my chair tomorrow morning and couldn't speak when the director cued we were live on air? I imagined myself stammering out my words, or blurting out something stupid, like goodbye instead of hello. I envisioned my face twitching as perspiration dripped down my forehead and left big obvious sweat puddles in my underarms. Would the station regret hiring me?

SAMANTHA: TUESDAY, SEPTEMBER 2

Cameron skipped work the following day and brewed coffee for us while I dropped the kids off at school.

When I came home, he offered me a steaming mug. I inhaled its rich scent of chocolatey undertones before setting it down on the kitchen counter.

"So when are you leaving us?" I asked, trying to sound matter-of-fact, hoping he would say he didn't want to go.

Cameron raised his eyebrows at me. "That was blunt."

"Well, no point beating around the bush." I smiled. "Pun intended."

"I don't want to leave. I love you. Besides, this probably isn't the best time right now after everything that happened with Sophia."

"Sophia already said she was sorry this morning before I dropped her off. If you want to stay, do it for all of us, not just Sophia."

He hesitated before speaking. "I could do that."

"But you don't want to keep up the charade. Not to mention, you have David." It was more of a question then a statement. I wanted him to fight for us, tell me our family was more important to him than dating men.

"I told you I wasn't seeing him anymore. Besides, David's a nice guy, but I was never in love." Cameron sighed, taking a sip of his coffee. "What would you like to happen?"

I pushed my fingers into my thighs, wanting to make this all stop. "Well, I don't know Cameron." I could hear the harsh edge in my voice creeping in despite my best effort to remain indifferent. "Do you want to stay here with us and continue to see David or whoever on the side? Would you rather pack your bags and get your own place? What is it that *you* want?"

"I want it all."

"Me too." I shot him a dirty look.

Cameron ran a hand through the layers of his tousled brown hair. "I think I'm ready to accept the consequences and live my life in honesty. So really it's whatever you want. I found an apartment. I can stay here or we can tell the kids we're separating for a while, and I can move into the new place. It's only five minutes from here. We could ease them into things if you want to do it that way."

"You just got back home. When did you find time to look for an apartment?"

"I drove by the complex on my drive back from Oregon, they have a *Live Here* sign up. I've been over there before so I know it's a nice place, and you can't beat the location. It's just an option Sam. I'll do whatever you want."

"So you want me to decide?" I asked, frustrated with his refusal to make a decision. Why did I have to choose between giving him permission to slink off or asking him to stay? If he wanted to leave us, couldn't he be the one to pull the trigger?

"I want you to know Sam, if we separate, you can live in this house for as long as my parents will allow it."

"Of course I'll stay in the house. And why would your parents kick us out? I'm raising their grandchildren." I felt my neck turning red. After losing Cameron, my biggest fear was giving up my home, a home that did not technically belong to us. I loved it here. "Why would you even say that? Don't I have enough stress right now?"

"I just wanted to make that clear, in case you were worried. Plus, I'll continue to fully support you and the kids. I'm not abandoning any of you."

Tears broke. So he really did want to leave. "I'm not ready Cameron. I don't want you to go."

"Then I'll stay." He rubbed my lower back. "We

can work on your timeline."

We sat and drank our coffee, taking careful, considered sips. Cameron studied the house as if he had forgotten what our place looked like. "Hey Sam, the floors look different. Did you have them professionally cleaned?"

An unexpected wave of rage filled my body. I picked up my mug and slammed it back onto the counter, watching the coffee slosh down the side. Brown streaks trailed across pristine white.

"Jesus, Samantha."

"Fuck you Cameron. Fuck you for doing this to me and to our children. You know what?" I pounded my fist on the countertop. "Fuck the timeline too. Here's what I want. I want *you* to stay here. I want *you* to take care of the kids and come up with a story, while I leave town for a while." My body surged with confidence. I was in charge again. Not Cameron.

"Where will you go?"

"To my mother's. I was supposed to fly out there in October anyway. Remember? You promised to switch your work schedule around to give me a couple of days to watch over her while she has her hysterectomy. I'll just extend my trip a little longer."

"That's a whole month away. Don't you want to stay here and work on things with Sophia first?"

I stood up from the chair and put my hands on my hips. "No. Sophia and I can talk tonight and then again when I get home. I'll fly out tomorrow after the kids are in school. I need to get away from this, to think, to figure things out. While I'm gone, you can decide how to handle the kids. This is your mess, Cameron. You clean it up."

I only hoped I wouldn't make things worse for myself back home in Klamath Falls. My skin crawled, I was itching for trouble, something to distract me from my pain.

NATALIE: TUESDAY, SEPTEMBER 2

It was my first real day on-air. An intern handed me my green tea while I took a few deep breaths. I told myself I was going to be fantastic. This was all about faking myself out. If I believed I could do it, I could do it. It was that simple.

We were going to be discussing the latest celebrity breakups and interviewing one of the housewives of Beverly Hills. Typical talk-show banter. No problem.

I had already been Louisa-fied with anchor-glam hair and makeup. The white blouse and olive pencil skirt I had chosen fit perfectly. This was my time to shine.

I was tucking in my blouse just so, when Inna nudged my shoulder. "Natalie, this is Alik, he's one of the production assistants who runs scripts and stuff around here. He has some updated sheets for you."

I looked up from my studio chair and glanced toward him. Alik was young, probably fresh out of college, with medium length dark brown hair, and a cleft chin.

"Hi," I smiled, not sure how to handle his unwavering stare and half smirk.

Something felt familiar about him, like we'd already met. I tried to remember where I might have seen him. Maybe he'd been around during my interview process, although I doubted it. He was too good looking to have forgotten.

"Hey Natalie, nice to meet you." He extended his hand, his skin an olive brown. Our palms touched, and I swallowed down my guilt as the moment between us lingered.

"Al-eh-k." I let the sound of his name roll around on my tongue. "Like Alec Baldwin?"

"Sort of. It's Armenian, from my mother's side of the family. Spelled A-L-I-K, same pronunciation."

I smiled without speaking. My immediate attraction to him set off silent alarms as loud as the fire drills at Lana's and Bens school.

"Okay Alik, enough with the introductions." The right side of Inna's upper lip lifted in irritation. "Just give Natalie her scripts."

I took the updated papers and watched him walk away. My eyes free to travel over his body unseen. The lean muscles in his back shifted under his fitted gray tee.

"Just ignore him." Inna waved her hand as if Alik was nothing more than an irritating housefly. "He's always trying to get involved in everyone's business. I'll run you your scripts from now on."

"Thanks." I smiled, somewhat disappointed, but also a little relieved. Something about him tempted shameful parts of me. He was someone I should stay away from.

My co-anchors, Dana and Jack, headed over to the stage

and took their seats on the living room set. Shaking off my last minute nerves, I stretched my neck from side to side before Louisa touched up our makeup. She laughed when I told her I thought the overhead lights were beginning to melt my eyelashes.

Jack gave me a pat on the knee. "How you doing Natalie? You want to do a dry run before the intro?"

"Sure, that would be great."

Dana shot me a fake smile while I did my best to ignore her.

"Great," Jack continued in a voice as rich as whiskey. "Let's get started."

After a few stumbles I felt ready to move forward—not that I had a choice. Kim gave us the time and let us know we were about to go live. I could hear the director begin his countdown in my ear...in three, two, one and ...."

"Good Morning LA" Jack beamed at the camera.

"Good Morning," Dana chimed in after him, her stone mask transformed into the face of an angel.

Jack took the lead. "Well we're back and as promised, we are sitting here now with the newest member of our team. Dana and I are pleased to introduce you to..."

"Wide shot, camera three. Go!" the director yelled in my earpiece.

"...Natalie Delisse. She is joining us today after flying in from sunny San Diego where she lives with her kindergartener son, Ben, and her adorable twelve-year-old daughter, Lana. Natalie's husband is rooting her on from his physical rehabilitation center where he is currently recovering from a major car accident that nearly took his life."

I felt my eyes grow wide. That last bit wasn't in the

script. I didn't know they were going to milk Mark's injuries right from the get-go. I should have known better.

"Thank you, Jack. I'm so happy to be here." I turned to camera three. "My audition tape was chosen from the thousands of wonderful videos sent in from stay-at-home moms across the nation. Women who were hoping to add their unique perspective to *Good Morning LA*. I'm proud to represent all of us here this morning."

"And rolling..." the director shouted once again in my ear. "Going to package, great job Natalie. Great job!"

They played a pre-produced story of me walking around my home and introducing my children. Ben and Lana said they were proud of their mommy. I talked about how excited I was to be joining the show and told our audience all about what I had to offer them from my wise mommy point-of-view. The producers had added a clip from my audition tape, as well as pictures of my husband before and after the car accident. All of it was set to sappy background music. I hoped the viewers weren't puking into their breakfasts over the schmaltziness of it all.

Some other person seemed to take over my body from there. I felt confident and engaged, as if I were a seasoned expert. All the little voices of doubt normally in my head went silent and I managed to keep from making any major on-air flubs. After we wrapped, Jack, Inna, and the rest of our team—everyone except Dana—gave me high fives. The phones lit up like blinking alarm clocks. Viewers said they loved me. I came across as friendly, likable and best of all, intelligent.

"You were awesome," Inna said to me as I walked toward my desk to check my cell phone. "I knew you were going to kick some ass. Congratulations."

I clutched her small curvaceous body into my arms for a huge hug. "Thank you Inna. I couldn't have done it without you and everyone else here. That was so much fun."

She squeezed me tight before she shimmied out of my embrace. "Pack up your things and let's get out of here. It's time to get you to the airport and back to your family. We can do this all over again on Wednesday."

Beaming back at her in gratitude, I turned and collected my purse and luggage, forcing any lingering thoughts of Alik to the back of my mind. I had nailed it. I had made it through my first day hosting a highly rated national morning talk show. I wondered if anyone on the plane would recognize me.

SAMANTHA: WEDNESDAY, OCTOBER 8

A crisp chill greeted me as the airport's automated glass doors whirred open. Clumps of unseasonably early snow lay in patches on dying yellow grass, slowly melting under the wide open sky. It was autumn in Oregon's Rogue Valley.

I exhaled in relief, at least the landscape looked the same. The airport itself was bigger and more modern than I remembered it. Mom told me it was either commit to major renovations or shut it down completely. The updates made in my absence felt like a betrayal, my past shifting its foundation behind my back.

Looking around, I spotted my mom. She sat in the driver's seat of her new no-nonsense white Subaru, parked curbside waiting for me.

"Hey Mom!" I waved, feeling my tough exterior begin to evaporate. I'd had to wait a full month longer than I wanted to make this trip. Cameron had stalled out on me, told me he couldn't take the time off work. I knew he was doing it on purpose to try and take the edge off my anger before I left, but it hadn't worked. I only felt more agitated, more amped up and desperate to break free.

The trunk popped open and a fifty-nine-year-old woman stepped out of the driver's side. Just like the airport, Mom had changed too, more wrinkles, more sagging under her eyes, an annoying reminder that none of us escapes the march of time.

She left the door open wide and walked toward me as her car chimed. Being within touching distance from her released an unexpected rush of emotion, that relief that it's finally safe to let go. My neck tightened while sobs caught in my throat.

"Mom," I wailed, waiting for her to put her arms around me and tell me everything was going to be okay.

"Oh Sammi." She pulled me in to her skinny frame. "I'm so glad you're home."

"Me too," I sniffled, tears wetting my cheeks. "I'm so sad, Mom."

"You will get through this. I promise." A handful of cars crept past us, their wheels wet with blackened sleet and melting snow. A flash of bright sunshine reflected off the moving metal and burned my eyes. Mom squeezed my arms and gently pulled away.

"Come on, let's get your luggage in the trunk."

"You look great," I warbled through the catches in my throat, using the side of my fist to swipe away the tears trailing down my face. I handed her my smallest bag, trying not to notice her disheveled sweater and tired blue jeans. As a child, I blamed my mom's dull appearance for Dad's disappearing act. If only she had put on some lip gloss or high heels, bought a new outfit every now and then, Dad might have stuck around.

"Are you staying longer than planned?" she joked, watching me load my two oversized suitcases into the trunk. "That has to be more than a week's worth of luggage."

"Better to over-prepare than under-prepare. I'm ready for Armageddon." After slamming the trunk shut, I tugged my coat on tighter. "Boy, it's cold can here for early October."

"Well it's nice and toasty in the car. I've got the heater set on high. Your seat warmer is on, too." Mom smiled with pride.

"I can't believe I'm here. I can't believe this is happening." New tears fought their way free. *Get it together Samantha. Quit your cry babying.* This was still a small town, hopefully no one I knew was around. I was a hideous mess.

"You mean you can't believe what's going on with Sophia, or with Cameron?" she asked.

"Both, but more Cameron. Sophia's just acting like a sixteen-year-old. She's hormonal."

"I was shocked too when you first told me," Mom said as we both slid inside her heated car and clicked on our seatbelts. "Cameron treated you like his greatest treasure before the kids came along. I thought any break you may have had in the romance department was just normal marriage stuff."

I rubbed my hands on my thighs, surprised she had picked up on any troubles in our marriage. "What kind of break?" I looked over at her now, feeling a little stronger.

"Nothing in particular. I don't know, there were a couple of times I called over the years when he was out late and you seemed frustrated, or he was spending more time with the kids than with you."

"Yeah, normal marriage stuff," I agreed, trying not to feel self-conscious about our less than perfect relationship. "Well, I'm happy to be home. It's been a long time."

We drove east along Highway 140 through winding mountain roads, past towering evergreens and into the endless blue horizon. A deer stood near the roadside, its eyes fixated on us. I had forgotten the striking beauty of my home state. Gazing out the windows, I marveled at the rugged geography as if for the first time. "Remind me why I ever left this place, Mom."

She laughed. "To find yourself. Remember? You were too big for this town? You wanted to take on the great wide world beyond."

I shook my head. "That's right. I remember now. The Great Samantha Foerster was going to tackle college and become a celebrated writer. I would marry Prince Charming and live the most envied life a girl could possibly imagine. No stepping foot upon Klamath Falls again until I became a living legend." I laughed despite my sorrow. "Where is my tiara?"

"I can see it. It's resting right upon your head, Princess, dripping in ten carat diamonds."

"Yeah right." I rubbed my hands on my thighs. "Nope, I married a gay guy and became a housewife with a runaway teenage daughter. Not so impressive."

Mom picked up speed. Sturdy pine trees swept into one big blur of green.

"Disappointed in me?"

"Not even a little bit." She patted my hand. "Everything is going to work out for the best. Sophia is going through a phase, and as for Cameron, no good comes from sticking with a man who isn't right for you. Especially not you. My daughter is feisty and smart, and the most determined person I know. You're going to come back from this better off than you could possibly imagine."

"Yeah, 'cause it worked out so well for you when Dad left. Right?" I bit my lip. I meant what I said, but I didn't mean to say it out loud.

"I told you before, you are *not* me. You live in a big city, you went to college, and married a man from a rich family. You have all sorts of possibilities I didn't have."

"Mom, I gave up my writing dreams and dropped out of Santa Cruz my junior year so I could start my photography empire. These days, I take the occasional family portrait at Balboa Park. Cameron's parents own our home and at this point, I'd be lucky to get a job working at Sears taking precious portraits of screaming, snot-nosed babies. Oh yeah, and instead of one child, I have three children."

Mom turned down the heater. "Such drama, Samantha. I'm sure his parents will let you live in their rental house for as long as you are raising their grandchildren. As for work, nobody has to know you didn't graduate. You're not applying to the CIA.

Just list a bachelor's degree on your resume. Make up some experience they can never fully verify. You'll get a good job and before you know it, someone new will sweep you off your feet and make everything better."

I tapped my fingers on my thigh. "Who are you Mother? Since when do you know anything about the CIA or lying on resumes? And as far as waiting for the next man to sweep in and rescue me, maybe I can take care of myself. Did you ever think of that?" I looked over at her with a smile to let her know I was at least half joking.

"I just want the best for you, that's all."

"We're almost to the lake now," I said, changing the subject. "I can't believe how fast this drive is going."

Twenty minutes later, we parked in the driveway of my childhood home, a drooping one story structure with faded green siding. The house, which blended in with the aging trees and shrubbery, was much smaller and even more worn than I remembered, an eight hundred square foot box, resting on an oversized lot. Dad had promised to build Mom a real ranch house on this land. Instead he skipped town.

I remembered how dark the place was. Coming here after school, I would talk on the phone with boys in the shadowed corners of my room, while Mom busted her butt as a waitress at the diner.

My fairy tale castle on Kingston Court was incomparable. I picked my kids up from top rated schools each day and drove them to volleyball practice and math tutors. We lounged at the pristine beach on the weekends with sand as soft as baking soda and splurged on shopping sprees at Del Mar's best boutiques.

This house and this life, resting under a dreary cloud-heavy sky, stood in sharp contrast.

"I'm sorry I haven't visited, Mom. I should have come with the kids when they flew out here last summer."

The deep lines around Mom's eyes crinkled as she looked at me. "That's okay. I love having those babies all to myself. This house isn't big enough for all of us anyway."

I opened the car door to get out. "I should have

come."

***

Mom settled into the couch with a romance book while I unpacked my suitcases and hung clothes in the matchbox sized closet of my old bedroom. Mom had set up bunk beds for the girls to share on their visits, while Gavin got the sagging pull out couch in the living room. I found it hard to believe I hadn't been here myself in twenty-four years.

Mom rapped her knuckles on my door.

"Yeah, come in."

She held out a small gift, wrapped in Christmas paper with a bow. "Remember this?" she asked.

I put my hands over my mouth in surprise. "You still have that?"

She nodded her head. "Well, I couldn't throw it away, could I? I found it a couple weeks ago when I was cleaning out the attic. It was covered in dust."

"Wow. I had forgotten all about it."

"Open it. Let's see what's inside of this thing once and for all." She handed the present out for me to take.

I shook my head as if she was offering spoiled food. "Maybe later."

"You've been saying that since he sent it to you more than thirty years ago. Let's just open the darn thing. Here." She thrust it back in my direction. "Take it."

I turned to unzip my luggage and hang a dress. "Mom, I just got here. Can we worry about that silly thing later? Just toss it on the bed."

"Promise me you won't leave it behind," she said. "I finally got the attic all straightened. It would be a shame to clutter it up again."

I turned toward her and watched her set it on the bottom bunk. "I promise."

Mom stepped out of the room, saying she was going back to her novel. Once I had everything in order, I took a seat on the lower bunk bed. Dust motes danced in the corner beside the door, and I couldn't help notice the window curtains had faded from a once bright yellow to near beige. The room smelled stale but comforting, familiar surroundings in a long neglected space.

I picked up the small box and twisted it in the single ray of dim sunlight fighting its way into my room. The ornate red and white wrapping paper still shimmered. Delicate ribbons remained curled in perfect loops. My father must have had it professionally wrapped before he put it in the mail. It was the last gift he had sent to me. Accepting this final token of his love would mean letting him go.

NATALIE: TUESDAY NIGHT
OCTOBER 14

I got to ask Gwyneth Paltrow all about her favorite children's recipes. Sarah Jessica Parker talked to me about her new book on raising twins. My first month of celebrity interviews had been exhilarating.

This week, Dana and I were sitting down with the uber-sexy Adam Levine.

Inna was not impressed. "I bet you're into him, aren't you?" she asked, snuggling deep into her plush couch. My chamomile tea had a spoonful of honey, just the way I liked it. Each week, on the nights before my Monday, Wednesday, and Friday shifts on the morning show, I made the two hour drive to Inna's place after preparing my kids dinner. This had become our pre-bedtime ritual—drinking tea and talking trash.

I looked at her over the steam rising from my UCLA mug. "Am I into Adam Levine? Seriously, is there a woman who isn't?"

Inna waved her hand as if to dismiss the notion. "I'd fuck him once and he'd go cry in the corner."

I laughed so hard, I spilled tea down my arm. No matter how much time we spent together, Inna's comments never failed to shock or amuse me. I was surprised at how much I enjoyed this quirky woman's company. "Okay, so if Adam doesn't do it for you, who would you like to have by your side?"

"Hmmm." She scrunched up her lips in thought. I dabbed at the tea dribbling down my arm while I waited for her answer.

"I would have to say ... Mark Wahlberg."

"Really? Marky Mark?" The former so-called rapper and Calvin Klein underwear model was not the guy I imagined Inna idealizing.

"Totally. He's hot, religious, flawless body, and a family man. He is *it*."

"You are a complicated woman, my friend." I shook my head and smiled.

"Not really. I just want a man with morals who takes care of his family." She set her mug down on a glass coaster resting on her large mahogany coffee table. Hang on a minute." She stood up and disappeared inside her kitchen's walk-in pantry. "Listen, it's been a long day and my kids are asleep," she called from the pantry. "You want to smoke a bowl before we call it a night?"

"Pot?" I asked, knowing the answer.

"Yeah, it's good weed. I got it from a friend of mine. He has the best shit." She emerged from the pantry holding a small pipe with a tiny seashell shaped bowl at the end of it.

I started to say no and then gave it another thought. Smoking out never really did much for me, but I figured *why not*. My time here in LA felt surreal, like I was living a double life. Why not let go of my inhabitations for one night?

"Sure," I said. "I haven't smoked since my trip to Amsterdam with Mark before the kids were born. It might bring back some good memories."

"Cool." She took a hit and blew seamless rings out of her O-shaped lips before passing me the lighter and pipe.

"Impressive."

She shrugged like it was nothing, but I could tell she appreciated the compliment. I ran the flame along the sweet smelling weed and inhaled deeply while she continued our conversation. "So, what about you? Who's your fantasy man? I've seen the way you check out Alik's ass. You don't have a thing for him do you?"

I coughed as I exhaled a small cloud of smoke. My arms and cheeks prickled with heat. "He's just so exotic looking, so intense."

"He's half Armenian. Go to Glendale and you'll find one on every corner." She twisted a lock of her hair and rolled her eyes to the ceiling. "I think it's his name. Alik Lucero. If he went by Tom Smith or Joe Johnson, no one would give him a second look."

"I don't think so." I laughed, already feeling the effects of the pot. "Anyway, it doesn't matter because I'm only looking. How old is he anyway?"

"Twenty-four." Inna grabbed a throw blanket off the side of the couch and laid it across her bare legs. She liked to wear nothing more than thong underwear and tank tops after her kids were in bed for the night. "You know he boned Dana Aldridge."

"The ice-queen?" I felt a renewed hatred for my self-absorbed co-host.

"Yep. He did us all a favor actually, pulled the stick out of her ass for a couple of weeks. It didn't last long though. They weren't serious."

"I thought he would have better standards."

"Why? You don't even know him. He's just some dude who runs scripts around the newsroom."

"Why don't you like him?"

"I don't get a good vibe off of him. If you feel like hooking up with him once or twice, that's cool. I just wouldn't want to see you fall for him."

I felt a shiver of excitement picturing the shape of his full lips pushing against mine, our tongues meeting and brushing against each other. It wasn't hard to imagine hooking up with Alik once or twice.

Inna took the pipe and lit the bowl, inhaling deep this time and holding her breath for several counts before exhaling. Long curls of smoke swirled over face. "I've only known you a short while, and I haven't ever met your husband, but you two seem like good people. Your marriage gives me hope."

"Yeah? Do you miss your husband?" I asked.

She tapped her index finger along the edge of the pipe and seemed to ponder the question. "Sometimes."

"You would like Mark. One of these days, when he's doing better, I'll have to introduce you to each other."

"What do you miss most about him?"

There were so many things. I missed the continuity he brought to my life. I missed his Sunday morning pancakes. I missed having someone around who took my side, and who would listen to me complain when I didn't feel well or the kids were being difficult. "I think the hardest part is falling asleep at night. His hand would latch on to some intimate part of my body, a breast, my inner thigh, a hip bone."

"And in the meantime," she coughed. "There's Alik."

"Can I tell you something?"

"What?" she asked.

"This is probably the pot talking, but when I first saw Alik it was so weird. It was like our souls knew each other."

"Oh Shit." Inna, red-eyed and glassy, let out a haggard raspy laugh.

My neck prickled and began to itch, breaking me

from my reverie. "What?"

"You are fucked." She laughed again.

I let my head fall back on a soft pillow and closed my eyes. My husband was sleeping in a rehabilitation facility. My mother-in-law was living at my house looking over my children. I was smoking weed in Los Angeles with my production assistant, preparing to interview Adam Levine in the morning, and fantasizing about a hot half-Armenian guy who may or may not be my soul mate. Who's life was I living?

NATALIE: THURSDAY, OCTOBER 16

I didn't want my overly involved mother-in-law asking any questions.

I left Kingston Court that evening in my every day mommy clothes with a plan to pull over at a familiar rest stop. My hands felt clammy and my heart raced when I saw the exit off the 5 North.

I clicked on my blinker and parked the car. Since the first time I met him, Alik and I had been exchanging furtive glances. Just looking at him made me feel like a nervous teenager. Toying with fantasies of Alik taking me on a first date or seducing me in the back of the newsroom distracted me during painful trips to visit Mark at rehab and from the monotonous day-to-day routine of pouring over homework with the kids, driving them from activity to activity, and carrying on pointless conversations with my mother-in-law. Thoughts of him often consumed me.

Inside the rest stop's swampy cinderblock bathroom stall, I changed into a slinky black dress. It was tight, with extra ruching around the hips to accentuate my curves. Besides my nights with Inna, I spent most of my evenings throwing my hair up in a bun to fold laundry or wash dishes after the kids went to bed. This was the first time I'd been out like this since the accident occurred five months ago.

Monday, just after the show wrapped, Alik found me in the break room and invited me to listen to his band tonight. Against my better judgment, I said yes.

After pulling off the 405 onto Wilshire Boulevard and crisscrossing numerous congested side streets, I glanced at the clock and realized I was early. Letting out a deep breath, I pulled into an empty parking lot situated behind the non-descript single-story nightclub.

The sun, just beginning to set, painted the sky pink, contrasting the older building's simple black matte exterior. I sat in my car, the moon roof open, windows rolled down, and enjoyed the balmy autumn air wrapping around me like delicate cashmere.

This was the type of weather that seduced Mark into moving to Southern California. He said he was home the day he set foot in San Diego. I had grown up here, and even so, the beauty of this state never failed to get me.

I pushed the driver's seat back and slipped on my

five inch heels. Mark loved the way these simple black shoes elongated my calves. Now he was living in rehab learning how to read and write, while I was putting on these stilettos to catch the attention of another man.

Guilt, upended by desire, tore at my conscience. I reminded myself that after three months in rehab, my husband still looked through me when I spoke to him. He barely remembered my name. I was only here to have a little fun, and I certainly deserved it.

Aside from one other vehicle, the lot was empty. I got out of my car and shut the door with a firm whoosh. Remembering a book I had forgotten in my glove compartment, I walked around to the passenger side to retrieve it. I figured I could browse through the pages again to prepare for my morning interview with the author.

I stood lost in thought, shuffling through my glove compartment when I heard his voice.

"Natalie?"

I poked my head out of the car in embarrassment and stood up straight. Alik was dressed in a black T-shirt and jeans, his dark brown hair swooped up a bit in the front giving him an edgy, rock-star appearance.

"Oh. Hey. What are you doing here so early?" I asked, shutting the passenger side, and wondering if he had checked me out from behind. The saleswoman had said my butt looked fantastic in this dress, a selling point that clinched the purchase.

"I always arrive early. I'm the drummer, I need

extra time to get set up." He pointed to the open trunk of his Jeep Cherokee, parked several empty spaces away from my car.

He moved closer to me, so close I could smell the soapy sandalwood scent of his skin. I wanted to bury my head into his chest and breathe him in. "Need some help?" I asked.

"In those heels?" he smirked. "You sure you want to be hauling heavy instruments?"

I smiled and looked at the ground. "I have flip flops in the car. Wait a second. I'll put them on and give you a hand." I opened my door again and searched under the seat, listening for his footsteps to walk back to his car. Instead he waited for me.

When I stood before him in more practical shoes, he gave me an approving nod. "You come prepared."

"I'm a mom." *Now that was sexy, remind him I'm a married mother of two.*

"Come on." He led me to his car and handed me a large cymbal and a drum stand to carry. I followed him through the parking lot to the back door, watching him carry some of the heavier pieces of his elaborate drum set.

"Hey Tom, we're here," Alik called out through the dingy low lit hallway. The place smelled of stale beer and lingering perspiration, like every college bar I'd ever trespassed.

"You've played here before?" I asked, changing my grip on the drum stand so I didn't accidently smack it against the wall.

"All the time." He looked back and watched me juggle his equipment. "You look pretty cute hauling my stuff around."

"Thanks," I said, at a near loss for words.

He walked to a small stage and set down two of his drums. "There's more in the car."

"I noticed," I said with a light laugh.

"I'm good though. You can hang out here while I get the rest."

"No way," I said, following him back to the vacant parking lot. "It gives me something to do while I wait for everyone else to show up."

"I can't promise that nothing's going to happen if you come back to the car with me." He looked back at me over his shoulder and smirked again as if he was joking.

Once everything was accounted for, Alik went to work setting up.

I stood near the would-be dance floor and watched him move on the stage. He placed the snare drum on its stand, his toned biceps flexing as he adjusted its height. Next he set up his stool. Alik fiddled with the height so his long legs were bent at just the right angle. Even *that* was sexy.

"I didn't realize how much detail went into something like this," I said, trying to sound interesting. What was this guy doing to me? I tingled at the thought of his hands running over my body instead of that drum set. He would grab my hips, pull me in close to him and tell me he needed to make love to me.

"I like doing it." He looked over at me. "It helps put me in the right state of mind."

"Can I get you something to drink?" I asked, needing to take a step away and compose myself. Standing there in that intimate space was getting the best of me.

"Sure, a Sam Adams would be great. You gonna get anything?"

I shook my head. "I'm good for now."

"Tom'll give it to you on the house. Order something if you like."

"Great. I'll let him know when I get thirsty."

As I rushed out to my car to put my heels back on, a mild evening breeze caressed my arms and legs. The final gasps of sunset, burnt oranges and blood reds, slipped off the horizon. I felt another deep blow of guilt. What was I doing here in this grungy LA night club lusting like a schoolgirl over a sexy young guy? I should have said no to his invitation, should have behaved like a proper married woman and gone straight to Inna's and called it a night.

It was too late. I was already here. My decision made. I chose to shake off the shame as I walked back inside. Tom gave me a beer for Alik and told me to make myself comfortable at any of the tables. After handing off the glass bottle, I chose a seat several paces back from the stage and pulled out my book, gazing over the top of the pages to watch him.

Alik put his bass drum in place and began attaching the legs, slipping them into the holes and tightening their hold by turning the knobs. As he leaned over, the bottom back of his T-shirt pulled up, revealing a sliver of his olive brown skin, and the sinuous curves of his lower back.

I imagined him at college parties stealing off to a quiet room after playing a set with his buddies, he would take off his clothes and make out with the girls who would taste the salt and sweat on his lips and fingers. These days, he probably had his choice of who he went home with at night. Anyone who set up his instruments with such care and devotion was sure to attract attention.

Alik sat on his stool and repositioned the drums around him while the rest of the band trailed in and began setting up. He took his sticks in his hands and looked at me with a mischievous smile, giving his drums a hard whack.

I forced my eyes back onto the pages of my book and thought of my husband, tried to remember when he was young and strong and full of promise. My co-workers would be here soon. I needed to appear casual, like I wasn't completely infatuated with Alik and trying to calm my racing heart.

***

In a darkened room, surrounded by Inna and my other co-workers, the lead singer of Alik's band shook her wild blonde hair and wailed into the microphone. The handful of people on the dance floor began to sway. Alik lifted his arms and beat the drums. Slow and steady, he created the timing for the rest of the group. Inna leaned over and squeezed my knee. "He's really good. You must be dying right now."

I ignored her and let my feet and body move to the rhythm of his music. Alik was better than I'd expected, the music flowed through his every move. His hair fell in his face and his lips puckered. I wished again I hadn't come tonight, hadn't heard the way he played.

Toward the final set, the free-spirited lead singer yanked Alik up to the front of the stage and handed him the microphone. I felt jealous of this young, creative woman, simply because she stood so close to him, and because she shared with him a special musical connection. I wanted to be the one standing there next to him in the spotlight. I could tell by the way she looked at Alik, she reveled in her proximity to him.

He stood awkwardly at the front of the stage, his head bowed down before looking up. The girl disappeared into the shadows. His audience cheered, encouraging him to sing.

Alik switched the microphone from his left hand to his right, while his eyes cut across the crowd and found mine. *Why is he looking at me? What is he thinking right now?* I felt raw and vulnerable, afraid he would lose his nerve, afraid he wouldn't.

The dark crowded room faded. I imagined him walking off the stage and coming to me. He would pull up a chair, look into my eyes, and tell me I'm the only woman he thinks about, that he wishes he met me first, before I was ever taken by another man.

Did he know that I was consumed by thoughts of him, that every time I left LA and confronted my real life, I daydreamed of making love to him? Alik was my fantasy, my escape, and in this moment, my singular desire.

I wanted to feel fully alive, to dive head first into the deep end, to feel that rush. Not only because of all the recent trauma, but also to make up for the last twelve years of dedicating myself without question to the people I loved most. In the past, I took pride in my sacrifices, certain they made me a better mother and wife. I had turned off some of my most basic female impulses, like buying the impractical fuchsia-colored high heels, staying out past midnight on a weekday, or flirting with the cute guy who was clearly checking me out.

As Alik opened his mouth and began to sing, his voice hushed the crowd. He sounded raspy, soothing, and thick at the bottom. He finished one song and began another. It was free flowing and upbeat. Inna and my co-workers shouted with enthusiasm. "Bring it," one of them yelled. My producer, Kim, drained her glass of wine and let out a loud yelp of appreciation.

"Killing it Alik!"

He was causing a scene and it only made me want him more.

I knew when his set was over he would come to our table and say hello. I knew that if he sat close to me, I would reach out and touch him, put my hand on his knee, brush my lips against his ear. I would ask him to walk me to my car—just the two of us. My longing would overtake my common sense.

I took a sip of beer and ran a hand through my hair. I was a grown woman. He was twenty-four-years-old. I had a budding career, school aged children, a life at risk. For him, I might amount to little more than his latest conquest. Maybe he didn't even really like me, forgot I existed when I wasn't around. Maybe I was a fun diversion while he made his way through his work days. Nothing more.

I didn't want to be another one of his flings nor did I want to do something I couldn't erase. Shouting into Inna's ear over the din of the music, I told her I would see her back at her place.

It was getting late. I didn't trust myself to stick around.

SAMANTHA: THURSDAY AFTERNOON OCTOBER 16

The surgeon who performed Mom's laparoscopic hysterectomy found me eyeing the clock in the waiting room. I set down my glossy gossip magazine with its detailed pros and cons of various celebrities butts and listened to her update, praying everything had gone well.

My mom's surgery was more complicated than expected. They found a suspicious tumor that needed to be tested for cancer. Mom would have to stay overnight, possibly two nights, before she was ready for discharge.

I speed walked to her room to see her for myself. Mom was sleeping, a strand of thinning hair lying across the bridge of her nose. I reached over and kissed her forehead, brushing aside the wayward hair. She was not allowed to have cancer. When a friend betrayed me, or Gavin got an A in citizenship, when I caught the flu, or Savanna broke a finger... I called my mom. How could any of those things matter if she didn't answer?

Sometime later, the quiet rap of knuckles on the half-closed door grabbed my attention. An older, petite woman with light brown hair and a bright, beautiful smile breezed inside the cramped room. She wore a flowing bohemian skirt and carried a lush bouquet of peonies.

"Elena."

"Samantha," she beamed.

I stood to greet her.

"I knew you'd be here," she said. "It's been so long."

Elena, my mom's dearest friend, set the fluffy pink flowers on the bedside table and gave me a tight hug.

She patted my back, and then held me out at arm's length, her tiny hands gripping my arms. "Look at you all grown up. You look like a supermodel."

I shook my head. "Thanks. You look gorgeous Elena. You haven't aged a day since I left."

"Please." She waved her hand in disagreement. "But seriously. Look at you. You know I'm usually not into blondes, that whole all American thing. But you have always had such a European flair about you. Very Sienna Miller. Very Boho-chic." She shooshed my hair. "So good to see you sweetie." She hugged me again before we sat down.

"So how did the surgery go?" she asked.

My head pounded. "The doctor said it went really well." It felt like a betrayal to tell her the truth. My mother should be the one to share that kind of information. Besides, the tumor was probably nothing. There was no reason to worry Elena.

"Thank God, right? What would we do without your mother? She's an angel."

"She is." I took another look at my mom, anxious for her to wake up. "So how have you been? I'm so sorry I haven't kept in better touch with you. My life just got ... so busy. I've missed you."

As a child, when Mom had to pull a double shift at work, or I needed another woman to confide in, Elena was there. She showed me how to use my first tampon. She taught me to match the color of my shoes to my pants rather than my top to make my legs look longer. Elena had been a second mother to me.

"Don't worry about it." She shook her head as if it were nothing.

Past scenes with Elena played in my mind. At twelve years old, when other adults noticed my long blonde hair or pretty blue eyes, Elena nurtured my artistic side. She listened to my stories and surprised me with a handmade leather bound journal. The first to encourage my writing, she insisted I write my stories down and promised they would be worth something someday.

As a teen, when other moms flung snide remarks about my various boyfriends, Elena dropped off college brochures and urged me to contemplate the future.

I stopped calling her after I failed to get into UC Santa Cruz's creative writing program. Then I actively ignored her care packages and notes when I dropped out of school completely. It was impossible to see her here today and ignore the sting of my poor choices.

I put my hand on top of hers, genuinely regretting losing touch with this special woman. From now on, I would show greater appreciation for the important women in my life. "So how is Emanuel, the world's most perfect husband?"

"Honestly, I'm not really happy with him right now." She snarled the corner of her lip in mock irritation. "He told me to get rid of this awesome table I found on the side of the road. The table is perfect, it just needs a little work and he can't see past that. I told him if I knew about his issues with style, I might have thought twice about spending the rest of my life with him."

I laughed despite my growing concerns for my mother. *Why was she still sleeping?* "You haven't changed a bit, Elena. I can't believe you're still living here. I thought for sure you would have packed your bags by now. Why didn't you ever move back to LA?"

"Forget it." She waved her hand like she was flapping away a foul odor. "My life is here, I need my freedom. I can't sit in traffic for an hour just to get a manicure."

Klamath Falls was not known for its rush hour delays.

Elena squeezed my hand. "Oh, that reminds me. There's this new place in town, Salon Sol. They give *amazing* mani/pedi's. Amazing. This place is primo. Not like the other loser businesses you're used to seeing around here. They even have a masseur. His name is Brett." She lifted her eyebrows in excitement. "Sha-bammy whammy. I'm telling you. You gotta check this guy out."

"Like now?" I joked.

"No, like the day after tomorrow. After your mom is back home and ready for some pampering. You could have a little mother/daughter day. Marla would love it."

"I think it's a great idea."

Mom stirred in her bed. I darted toward her side, willing her to open her eyes.

"Is everything okay?" Elena's eyes shifted between my mother and me.

"Sure. Just eager for her to wake up. I haven't gotten to spend much time with her yet."

"Start visiting a little more often," she nudged. "Listen, I'm on a mission. I've got to run home and get dinner going before my guests arrive. I made the mistake of scheduling a little party this evening. Tell your mom I stopped by. I'll be back again tomorrow." Elena stood to leave.

"But you just got here," I protested, nervous about

being alone when Mom first woke up.

"I know. But I gotta run. Give your mom my love, and we'll catch up tomorrow."

I walked toward Elena and gave her a hug. "Thanks for coming by. I know it will mean a lot to her."

When the nurses finally woke my mom so she could eat, she didn't seem at all fazed by the possibility of a cancerous tumor, or by my down pouring of tears. She also didn't want to hear my tirade about life's unfairness and what it owed me. Instead she insisted I head home to feed her cranky old cat Earl. Against my better judgment, I left her with my stack of tabloid magazines and promised to be back first thing in the morning.

***

Sorrow followed me home like an abandoned dog. It was only six o'clock and the last thing I needed was time alone to think. I didn't want to dwell on my past mistakes, nor did I want to give much thought to my present or future. I fed Earl, made myself a peanut butter sandwich, and called my kids.

As soon as we said goodbye, I began to feel restless again. After checking my voicemails, I scrolled through the contacts on my cell phone. I had run into my ex-boyfriend from high school at the small grocery store in town the other day. Bobby had passed me his number and encouraged me to give him a call. He was renting a small house nearby and wanted to catch up.

I sent him a text to see what he was up to for the night. Within seconds my phone chimed with his response.

Waiting to hear from you. Come over.

I only hesitated for a second.

SAMANTHA: THURSDAY NIGHT
OCTOBER 16

I stood at the threshold of my ex-boyfriend's opened front door and peeked inside his tiny, tattered family room. "So this is where you're living now Bobby?"

"Temporarily," he said, running his hand through his copious dirty-blond hair. I tried not to stare at him. Dressed in an old pair of blue jeans and a button down flannel, Bobby looked so grown up standing there in his very own place, even sexier than when we were kids and he was the hottest guy in school.

"Come on in." He motioned with his hand. "I'm just staying here while I figure out what's going to happen with the wife." He was staying at the Rileys' old place. He'd said they'd held on to it when they moved up the hill.

I scanned the threadbare sofa covered in a red plaid blanket. An old-school television with bunny ear antennas rested on a plastic crate opposite the couch. "It's just the way I remember it." Even the faint Pine-Sol scent of the place brought back memories. "Is the lock on the back door still broken?"

Bobby chuckled, the laugh lines crinkling around his dark green eyes. "Yeah, not too much has changed around here."

Pushing up the sleeves of my floral blouse, I toyed with my ponytail and waited for him to offer me something to drink. Then I realized he probably wouldn't think of it. "So what is the deal with your wife?"

"She kicked me out. My old lady was hooking up with some other dude and now she thinks he's the one. She said I hadn't taken her out on a real date in twenty years and I don't know a thing about romance."

"Nice," I smiled. "Still a real Don Juan, aren't ya Big B?" I picked up a crumpled car magazine resting on the side of the couch and then set it back down. "So, are you going to offer me a beer? It's been a long day."

He shook his head. "And I see you still have no problem putting me in my place, Sammi Jane. Yeah, I picked up your old favorite after I ran into you at the store. I've got some Rolling Rocks chillin' in the fridge."

I hadn't touched a Rolling Rock since high school.

"I feel so special," I smirked.

"You should, Princess. I don't plan ahead for just anybody." Bobby headed toward the kitchen. Following behind him, I took a seat at an old Formica table and pushed out a chair for him with my toes. Leaning inside the fridge a little further, he gave me an ideal shot of his tight, rounded ass. I watched as he rummaged through the myriad of Styrofoam take-out boxes, making his way to the beer.

"Never did learn to cook did you?" I asked.

"I can throw a few things together. Just don't have anyone to do it for right now. I ordered out last night and got enough for leftovers is all."

I shook my head, thinking about all the lunches I missed out on in high school because I was busy doing other things with Bobby. "So what have you been up to since I left town?"

"Nothing as exciting as you. I hear you graduated from Santa Cruz and married yourself a rich man. Word is, you bought a swanky home by the beach and had a couple of kids."

"Three actually. But that about sums it up." I leaned back in my seat. I liked his assessment of my life. It was clean and simple and good.

Bobby popped open our bottles and sat down in the chair I'd pushed out for him. "Gotta say Sammi, you still look just like the girl I fell in love with all those years ago. I should have married you while I had the chance."

I took a swig of beer. "Too bad you stuck your hands in someone else's panties. That was a dumb move Bobby."

He didn't seem bothered. "I was just being an idiot. Your girl Tracy and her buddy Kellee Krogstad wanted to get it on with me at the same time. What was I supposed to do? I'd never had a threesome before."

My eyebrows shot up at the memory. "I thought you said it never happened. Are you admitting to your crime?"

He brushed his hand through his full head of hair. "Yeah well, I was telling you the truth. It never happened. They changed their minds at the last minute. I think Tracy was just trying to one up you. You know, show the other girls she could have me if she wanted."

"Yeah, if another girl was along for the ride." I could feel my blood pressure rise. "She was such a nasty little bitch." After all these years, it still made me angry. "So what happened? Did you show up and they backed out?"

"No, Tracy told me to come pick her up first, and then we ended up driving out to the woods. She said Kellee changed her mind but she was more than ready to make it up to me. I didn't want to hurt your feelings, but I was all revved up and ready to go. I couldn't just turn around and bring her back home." He looked at me like an injured child. "It was a stupid mistake."

"Your loss." I brushed an old crumb off the scratched table. "I had a threesome in college. It was pretty cool."

"No way!" His knee bumped the bottom of the table. "With another chick or two dudes?"

"Another girl. We gave the guy quite the show." I grinned, preparing to describe in explicit detail the type of tryst that would really blow his mind.

"Go on, I'm listening."

"It was me and my college roommate, a redhead with double D's. We were rolling on Ecstasy, hanging out with her hot boyfriend." I flashed a wicked smile at Bobby, registering his reaction. He leaned forward with interest.

"God, it was the greatest feeling, just being lost in a haze of sex. Her milky white skin felt like the softest silk. I'd never been with a woman. It was so new and exciting. I wanted to explore her whole body while he watched."

Pushing back in my chair, I did my best to torture Bobby, to punish him for not treating me better when he had the chance. "I ran my fingers through her hair, put her hands down my panties. We were like hungry little bears, pawing each other, feeling the sensation of our warm bodies pressed together. I could have spent all night with her, but he was begging us to give him some love." I stopped to make sure Bobby was still paying attention.

"And?" he said.

"The rest is too much to share. It was good though. Something I'll never forget."

"Lucky bastard."

I nodded my head. "Yeah, once it was over, the poor guy was ready to sell off his own sister in exchange for a second go around. My roommate told him to hold on to the memory, it was a onetime deal."

"Boy, you always knew how to have a good time." He leaned in close, leaving me with the lingering scent of fresh earth and pine trees on his worn flannel shirt. "You wouldn't be interested in trying it out again would you? For old times' sake?"

For a second, I considered it. After years of mediocre sex with my gay husband, doing something dirty and memorable felt enticing. If I was going to break it off with Cameron, why not do it big?

Then I thought of the size of this small town, and of my mother. Nothing stayed a secret around here. "I don't think so. You lost out on that opportunity when you fucked Tracy Morley. No threesomes for you."

"Damn." He shook his head in jest.

"What ever happened to her anyway?"

"Tracy? Last I heard she was on her sixth kid. One of her exes got custody of the first three. The newest batch lives with her in some trailer park out in Arizona."

"Yep." I smirked, feeling incredibly smug. "Too bad she's not around anymore. I bet she looks smokin' hot."

"I was just kidding anyway. I'm a man now, and I wouldn't want to share you with anyone else. No matter what the other chick looked like."

"Oh, you're so mature now? Ready to show me some proper respect?" I laughed.

"You better believe it." He stood up from his chair and headed toward the fridge. "Want another beer?"

One more led to another, and then another. Bobby ran out for replenishments and by the time the moon was in danger of disappearing behind the glare of the sun, we were both good and drunk. I felt transported. I was seventeen-years-old all over again.

He made his move while we were sitting on the tattered couch. Bobby leaned in, pushing me backward and kissing me hard as I wrapped my legs around his waist. He tasted like warm alcohol and cigarettes. He kissed like a man who wanted a woman. His coarse stubble rubbed my chin and lips raw, and I liked it.

"God, Bobby. I forgot how good you could make me feel."

He slipped off my hair-tie and released my pony tail, moaning in my ear. "I've been dreaming of having you again ever since you left."

His erection pushed against my thigh. I felt the warmth of his hand travel up my blouse and under my bra. Bobby breathed in deeply. "You smell so good. I missed the way you smell, Sammi."

I moaned underneath him. My hands roamed toward the front of his waist and undid the button of his jeans. I needed this, to get lost in my senses, escape into my former self, no thoughts, no concern for who or what I was supposed to be.

"Come on girl," he lifted me up with ease. "I'm taking you to bed."

Bobby carried me to his musty bedroom and laid me down in a hurry, pressing the weight of his broad body against mine.

I slid down his zipper and reached inside his pants. "Just the way I remembered it." I smiled at him.

He rolled off of me and onto his back, pulling off his jeans. I took off my own pants and sat on top of him, straddling his waist and admiring his hard flat stomach. My body demanded more.

I unbuttoned my top as he watched and then asked him to strip off his own shirt. Trying to restrain myself, I ran my fingers through his chest hair. "Do you have anything?"

"What do you mean?" he asked as he placed his hands on my hips.

"Protection."

His eyes widened in surprise. "We never needed any of that before." He slipped his finger inside my panties and smiled.

"Yeah. Well, I've learned my lesson. I brought something with me just in case. Want me to get it from my purse?"

"Sure, I guess."

I moved off him and made my way back to the living room, wishing it wasn't necessary to have to bring up the subject in the first place. It broke the mood and stole some of the spontaneity.

Back in the bed, I tried to recreate the moment. I kissed the different angles of his face and laid my breasts across his chest, moving them down his stomach, kissing him as I got closer to his hips.

"That's it Sammi. I'm taking you now." He rolled me over on to my back. Placing himself on top, he spread my legs with his knee, and moved himself inside me. Now I really felt like we were back in high school, back to the same old missionary position. He didn't even give me time to go down on him, let alone consider reciprocating. Did his routine never change? It felt so good when we were kissing each other. I had forgotten the rest of the details, the lack of ingenuity or desire to truly please his partner.

Digging my nails into his back, I tried to enjoy it. He felt good as he moved inside me and I liked the way he tensed up with pleasure during his orgasm.

I didn't get mine, but after he collapsed beside me in a state of bliss, I pretended I did just so the thing could be over. It occurred to me this was probably the real reason I broke up with him all those years ago. Just like Cameron, making love to Bobby wasn't really about pleasing me. I hadn't been this man's, or any other man's top priority.

A patch of light shined across my face. This was my cue to leave. I leaned over and gave Bobby a kiss on his shoulder. Then I sat up to gather my clothes.

"I've got to get going if I want to be back at the

hospital before my mom wakes up."

He slid his warm arm around my bare waist. "Why don't you stay?"

"Because, I need to be there when she wakes up. It's bad enough I let her talk me into leaving her all night."

"Come back when you're done with visiting hours?"

I rested my hand on top of his and looked around the room. Bare, scuffed walls encased the lonely space. A beat up chest of drawers rested against the back wall while dust gathered on the bent, beige-colored mini blinds.

I shook my head. "This can't happen again."

"Why? I've got plenty more left for you."

"How irresistible."

"I'm serious. I could take you out on a real date. We can get dressed up and go somewhere special."

"Hmm." I looked at the framed picture on his chest of drawers, the only picture on display in the entire house. "Pretty girl."

Bobby laid back down on the bed, placed his free hand under his head and looked over at the photograph. "Sure is. That's my Madison. Going into high school next year."

I noticed the flex in his chest and bicep as he turned back to me. "Same age as when I met you. Better watch out Bobby." I smiled. "Your little girl is gonna be a beauty."

"She'd like you."

"I'm sure I'd like her too."

"You're leaving for good, aren't you?"

I was sober now and it was time to get out. "I'm going to visit my mom. I'm sure we'll bump into each other before I take off. It's not that big a town."

He traced the palm of my hand with his finger. It wasn't fair to use him like this, nor was it working very well. Leaning over, I gave Bobby another light kiss, on the cheek this time and jumped out of bed before he could say another word.

NATALIE: FRIDAY, OCTOBER 17

Alik found me in the break room after the morning show. I sat at a small round table eating a quick breakfast of bagel and cream cheese before I got on the road for the two hour drive home.

He poured a cup of coffee and ambled toward me. Small curls of steam rose from his mug. We were alone. A television buzzed the local news on the countertop near the microwave. Overhead lights cast an ugly fluorescent hue on my skin, his skin, my food and his coffee cup. My head felt heavy, tired of living in limbo. My body demanded rest.

"You took off last night. I didn't see you after the gig." Alik peeked down at me and then into his coffee mug.

"It was getting kind of late. I was worried I might

not be able to wake up this morning if I stayed much longer."

"Thanks for coming out." He looked me in the eyes.

I was trapped in his gaze. My heartbeat accelerated, and my arms and neck prickled with heat. "Of course," I nodded, swallowing a bite of my bagel and fumbling with the thin paper napkin. "I wanted to be there. You're very talented, but I'm sure you already know that."

He took a seat across from me. "I'm glad you think so."

"I do. You seemed a little nervous before you sang, but you really impressed the crowd." I wanted to say more, wanted to tell him how the sound of his voice sucked away the darkness, how I wanted to fold myself into his lyrics.

Fortunately, I was aware these thoughts could land me on some sort of secret stalker's list or at the very least win me a prime seat at any Cheaters' Anonymous group meeting. Still, I couldn't resist the temptation of him so close. I slid my hand across the table and placed it on top of his, touching him for the first time. "Alik?"

He looked at our hands, my pale white skin atop his, warm and tanned.

"Thank you for including me."

Before he could respond, Inna sauntered into the room and strode by our table. She afforded me a smile, watching me pull my hand away from Alik's. "Great show today. You slayed that senator. I've never seen a politician look so afraid."

"Thanks Inna. I just got so fired up when he mentioned cutbacks in our schools. I know it was supposed to be Dana's interview, but I had to say something. He mentioned it like it was no big deal, like it was all part of the greater good. It's so shortsighted."

"Well you really kicked the segment up a notch," Inna continued. "He obviously had no clue our mommy co-host has worked around enough reporters to ask the tough questions."

Alik slid back in his chair and sipped his coffee. "Natalie kills it on every show. It's only a matter of time before they have her go full-time."

"Nonsense," I said, feeling more than a little embarrassed but also flattered.

"I mean it," Alik continued. "I heard Dana's shopping her resume tape, looking for a more 'interesting' position at someplace more 'prestigious'."

I set down my bagel. "Dana has nothing to worry about. I've only been here a little over a month and I haven't heard a single word from any of the higher ups about a promotion. Even if it were true, I couldn't accept the job."

"Why not?" Alik asked, sitting a little straighter in his chair.

"Because I don't live here. I can't drive up to Los Angeles every night and back down to San Diego every morning. Three days a week is enough."

"I know a good realtor," Alik tucked a lock of his hair behind his ear.

"Inna, will you tell him that when you have children you can't pick up and move like it's no big deal." I looked over at her for support.

Inna poured a cup of coffee and mixed in some sugar. "I also heard they're thinking about offering you a promotion once you're a little more seasoned. The ratings have gone way up since you started. I think you'd be crazy not to take it."

I rubbed my thumb nail across my teeth. "Thanks for letting me know." I shot her a dirty look.

She stared right back at me. "I would have told you last night, but you took off so early."

"Whose side are you on here my friend?" I felt so much bolder about speaking my mind when I was in work mode. "Anyway, it doesn't really matter. There's no way I could take that position. My kids adore their schools. The majority of our friends are in San Diego. Plus, Mark has been making progress in rehab. I couldn't just uproot everyone because I wanted to work an extra two days a week."

Inna sat down, filling the space between Alik and me. "It wouldn't just be an extra two days of work. It would be a big step up in prestige and salary. Forget about the whole stay-at-home mom from cute little San Diego sharing her perspective. You would be a real player, in a major market, on a nationally syndicated talk show. That's not something to take lightly, *my friend*. Think about it before you get the call. Consider what it could mean for your career."

On the drive home, I did give a potential promotion quite a bit of thought. It was fun to imagine a whole new lifestyle, more respect, easier access to all of the exciting LA events, a bigger paycheck. My twenty-two-year-old self would have been beside herself with delight. But I wasn't twenty-two-years-old. Everything I had said about moving my family to Los Angeles right now was true. There was also Alik. How could I resist my attraction to him, and remain faithful to my husband if I lived in the same town and saw him at work Monday through Friday?

NATALIE: FRIDAY, LATE MORNING
OCTOBER 17

Elizabeth came down the stairs fresh from the shower, her face rigid, wringing her hands full of nervous energy. "Morning. Welcome back home."

"Thanks."

"I wanted to tell you before I forgot, one of your neighbor friends dropped by yesterday evening after you left town. A fuller figured gal, very chatty?"

"Beth?" I pulled a cereal bar out of the pantry and peeled back the wrapper.

"Yes, that's the one. She stopped in to see what you were up to. She said you had your hair all done up and makeup on like you were going somewhere special. She wanted to know if you were cheating on her with your glamorous new LA girlfriends." Elizabeth eyed me up, no doubt looking for signs of guilt.

I took a large bite of my bar and shook my head in disbelief. "Beth is so funny. I had makeup on from a meeting I had with Ben's teacher. Nothing exciting." The lie rolled off my tongue far too easily.

"Well, be sure to let her know that next time you see her."

"Will do Elizabeth." I polished off my bar. "That all?"

She straightened the gold bracelet on her wrist. "Do you have a moment?"

My stomach twisted into a tight knot. I was not in the mood to skirt around the issue of Alik. One lie per day was enough. "Will it take long? I wanted to go visit Mark at rehab while the kids are at school."

Elizabeth sat down on the family room couch and smoothed the soft suede beside her. "There's something you need to know."

"You can just go ahead and tell me, Elizabeth." I walked toward the kitchen counter to put some distance between us. Even though the housekeeper was coming later in the afternoon, I tore a paper towel off its roll and wet it with warm water and a dollop of dish soap. I wanted to scrub the granite countertop while we talked. It would be better to stay on my feet, do something physical to absorb the blow of whatever she had to say.

"You know I've been telling you about Ben, his rebellious behavior, the way he doesn't listen to me."

My entire body stiffened. She could point out my

flaws, but I wouldn't let her go after my son. "Yes."

"Well his kindergarten teacher mentioned to me that he separates himself from his classmates sometimes. He goes in the corner and rocks his body. He makes strange noises and says he wants to be left alone."

I scrubbed harder, mangling the paper towel in the process. Elizabeth and I had gone over this before. It bothered me that she was harping on the issue. "You know he's been diagnosed with an anxiety disorder. When he gets overwhelmed, he self soothes by rocking himself. It's normal for him." I said as I walked over to grab another paper towel.

"I guess," she relented before revving up once again. "Well yesterday afternoon, your neighbor Marina dropped by for a visit. She brought over her new puppy for Lana and Ben to meet."

"She mentioned she was going to do that," I nodded, moving to the other end of the counter and picking at a dried ring of vanilla frosting. Glancing up at her, I gave her a tight smile. "I bet the kids were in heaven. They love puppies and chocolate labs are the cutest."

"They were. Lana took to little Murphy right away. So did Ben. He couldn't get enough of the dog. He lay on the floor, let it run up and down his body, lick his face, nip his fingers. He seemed quite taken with the dog."

I wished Elizabeth would get to the point of her

story. While I was the first to admit none of us would be coping as well without her, the woman could still work a nerve. Looking her straight in the eyes now, I spoke. "It sounds like it was a successful visit. I'm glad Marina brought Murphy over."

"Well, yes." She rubbed her hands across her skirt. "I'm not going to sugar coat this. I'm just going to tell you straight out what Ben said."

I raised an eyebrow at her, waiting for her to continue.

"He said, 'I love this dog so much I would let him lick me anywhere ... well except for my ...'" Elizabeth stopped.

"Expect for his what?"

"Except for his *dick*. He said he would let that puppy lick him anywhere besides his *dick*."

Resuming my scrubbing, I couldn't hold back a slight giggle. Ben did say the strangest things sometimes. I could only imagine the horrified looks of disbelief on Elizabeth's and Marinas faces when he said it.

"That is just not acceptable behavior. I know you said he has an anxiety disorder, but he seems more than just nervous to me, he's downright disrespectful. I had to wash his mouth out with soap."

I stopped my cleaning. "You did what?"

"I didn't have a choice. He needed to know what he said was wrong. He's a child who could benefit from a firm hand, someone to make it clear what is right and what is wrong. I had to do something he would remember."

My hands trembled. Elizabeth had no right to put poison in my child's mouth, to punish him for something he said in innocence.

"He's fine Elizabeth. Not all children fit the mold. He's five-years-old, and he says what's on his mind. He doesn't do it to be bad or get attention. He just thinks differently." I threw away my paper towel with force and wrapped my hair into a tight bun. "I'm going to take a shower." My curt tone polluted the air between us.

"I'll just make my breakfast then." She stayed seated on the sofa. "I organized the pantry yesterday while the children were at school. I hope I didn't throw away anything important."

I didn't give a damn whether or not she cleaned out the pantry. None of her help gave Elizabeth the right to take over the job of parenting my child. "Elizabeth, thank you for being here and for taking care of Lana and Ben while I'm at work. We all appreciate you more than I can say." I stopped at the stair rail and looked at her. "Also, please don't ever put soap in my child's mouth again. It's not how Mark and I discipline. There's no spanking and there's no soap. We talk to our children. We give them time outs when necessary."

Elizabeth tended to a piece of invisible lint on her prim white cotton skirt. "Maybe he needs more than a time out."

I grasped the handrail a little tighter. "I'm going upstairs now."

***

I made sure the water was as hot as possible, eager to burn the conversation with Elizabeth off of me. Steam rose in the glass encasement and fogged the mirror. Elizabeth's old-fashioned ideas of right and wrong were archaic and unyielding. They left no breathing room for a child who was unique.

I stepped inside the shower and watched my thighs turn cherry red. Ben's school psychologist had mentioned autism after evaluating him in his pre-school classroom. I told her that was not possible. I knew what autism was, I had watched those terrifying exposés on the horrors of a disorder that stole a child's ability to communicate or connect with loved ones. My son adored his parents, worried about his older sister. He spoke before he was a year old and hadn't shut his mouth since. The school therapist backed down. She said she was sure I was right, Ben probably just suffered from separation anxiety.

I took him to a supremely expensive, out of pocket psychiatrist, just to be sure. Mark and I sat on her bloated couch in a cramped, humid office with a view of the Pacific Ocean while Ben played with toys in the waiting room. We answered all her questions, regurgitated our family history. Next we sat and watched while she spoke with Ben. She asked him questions, observed him, and typed an inordinate number of notes on her laptop.

When we finished, she mentioned Obsessive Compulsive Disorder or the possibility of autism. She suggested we treat the OCD, a type of anxiety disorder, and then reevaluate. Ben went on Prozac for his nervousness and the medication made a big difference. We moved on.

Flames of water pelted my back. I turned to reach for the shampoo and let the full force of the spray strike my chest. I twisted the handle further left. More heat. Ben had been doing worse lately. I had attributed it to his father's accident, to my going back to work, to his annoying grandmother living with us.

My mom mailed me a newspaper clipping on autism recently which listed a bunch of symptoms that had made me think of Ben. *High sensitivity*. Ben hated getting haircuts. He had a complete meltdown every time I tried to take him to the salon. I couldn't turn up the radio without him holding his ears and crying. *Unusual movement, inability to sleep, inappropriate responses in social situations*. Ben's head banging had become more intense. He couldn't sleep through the night. His teacher had already sent him to the office twice this year. Once for grabbing her breasts, a second time for telling a kid he looked retarded.

I thought of the way he clung to me sometimes. The way he rubbed his head up and down my arms and stomach like a cat, sniffing me, smelling me, and then rubbing and smelling himself. My own body would go rigid in response. His touch could make my skin crawl. A mother wasn't supposed to feel that way about her child.

I shut off the water and marched over to my bedroom door to make sure it was locked, dripping puddles of water off my naked body along the way. Then, as tears blurred my vision, I stomped over to my bed and began beating the helpless pillow. Taking turns, using each fist, I hit harder and harder. I bent over and shoved my head into the fattest one and sobbed until I screamed. I needed to break things, but I didn't want to make a scene with my mother-in-law.

Inside the walk-in-closet, I proceeded to tear every piece of clothing off its hanger. Cheap temporary drawers went next. I pulled out the plastic bins holding my bras and underwear and old panty hose, all of my socks and scarves and faded, useless bathing suits, gutting each of the little compartments, and flinging their contents against the wall. Collapsing on the soft piles of clothes, I ripped the buttons off of each one of Mark's dress shirts. He didn't need them. He never left his room at rehab and his mother helped him get dressed.

Elizabeth had no right to imply there was something wrong with my son. She ought to have kept her soap and her opinions to herself. Our family had enough problems.

Standing up, I placed an old silk blouse under my bare foot, pulling and tugging, wrenching the soft luxurious material until it burst its seams. The resilient, purple fabric tore in one long nasty rip.

Exhausted, I rubbed the frayed blouse across my face, drying my tears, and finding comfort in its silky caress. *Everything is good. Everything will work itself out. I'm overreacting.*

Digging through the tangled, pathetic piles of abused clothing, I found socks, underwear, and a pretty black lace bra. An old cotton sundress lay crumpled in a corner. I put on some makeup and combed my hair.

As I left the house, Elizabeth asked if I was all right. Even with makeup, the puffy welts under my eyes must have been hard to miss. I told her I was fine.

SAMANTHA: MONDAY AFTERNOON
OCTOBER 27

I took Elena's suggestion. With a quick phone call, I booked an appointment for my mom and myself at Salon Sol. A week and a half had passed since her surgery and the results on her tumor had come back. It was benign. I wanted to celebrate.

For Mom, I reserved a deluxe mani/pedi. For me, a massage with the hot masseur Elena had gushed about.

Stepping inside the serene reception area right around noon, we were both ready for a little TLC. I checked us in with the cheerful brunette girl at the desk while Mom poured us glasses of water with cucumber. As soon as I took a seat next to her, a twenty-something-year-old guy with a beautiful tan body and long legs came out of the hallway and called my name.

"Samantha Chase?"

"Yes?"

"I'm Brett, I'll be your massage therapist today."

Elena was right. Sha-bammy whammy. Standing at least six feet, with an eager smile and a strong jaw line, Brett was ridiculously easy on the eyes. I imagined what lay beneath his powder blue Salon Sol shirt and khaki pants.

Mom whispered in my ear, "Lucky you."

I smiled back at her before gathering my purse and following this gorgeous man to the small room at the far end of the salon.

"You can set your things down in this chair here Samantha." He pointed to a plain wooden seat in the corner. The space was dimly lit. Soft rainforest sounds of trickling water and birds chirping piped in through the overhead speakers. A purple candle flickered on the black granite countertop, and the calming scent of lavender filled the cozy room.

"Romantic scene." I batted my Latisse-enhanced eyelashes. "You shouldn't have gone to so much trouble."

"Only the best for my favorite clients." Brett's chocolate brown eyes held mine as he smiled.

"Am I your favorite already?" I asked, trying to hide my delight.

"Absolutely. I have a good feeling about our session. Before I step out to let you undress, what kind of massage are you interested in today?"

"A good one. Something to really work out all the

stress I've been carrying."

"Where do you carry most of your tension?" he asked.

"Everywhere."

"Okay, then we'll do a full body massage. I'll work harder on any areas I sense you need it most."

"That sounds wonderful," I said with a flirtatious grin.

Brett looked me in the eyes with a hint of a smile and then took a step toward the door. "I'm going to wait outside while you undress. Feel free to slip under the sheets when you're ready. I'll knock on the door in a few minutes."

"Will do, Brett."

After he left, I took my time. Once I had carefully folded my clothes, placing my delicate underthings on the top for Brett to see, I slid under the warm cotton covers and waited for him. When he knocked, I asked him to come inside.

"Are you ready Ms. Chase?" he asked in a soothing voice as he reentered the room.

"What happened to calling me Samantha?" I teased from between the opening in the face rest.

"Are you ready Samantha?" he asked in a throaty whisper.

I pulled my hair to the side, exposing the nape of my neck. "All set."

"Perfect." Gently, he pushed the sheet down to just above my tail bone. He ran his warm palms up along my back to my shoulders before he stopped to apply lavender scented oil to his hands. "You have really awesome skin."

"Thanks." I felt my cheeks flush. "So what brings you here to Klamath Falls anyway? I don't get the feeling you're a local."

"You don't?" His voice raised an ever so slight octave in the quiet room. He seemed pleased. "Ah well, I've only been here for about a year now. I moved from Utah to become a ski instructor. Things slow down when the snow melts, so I thought it would be cool to put my massage therapy experience to use," he said as he worked out the knots in my upper back.

"One more month 'til ski season. I used to count the days until it was time to officially hit the slopes." I felt him continue to work his fingers down to the lower half of my back. "Mmmm, yes. Late November, just a couple more weeks unless the snowfall waits until December.

"I can't wait," he said. "Being here, doing what I'm doing, it's the best of both worlds. You know?" He pushed his palms deeper into my back.

"Your hands feel fantastic Brett."

"I'm glad you're enjoying yourself. You really needed this, your body is way too tense for such a sexy woman." He pulled the sheet upward exposing just one foot. Pressing his strong fingers in between each of my toes, he pushed them back to loosen the joints. The soft music lulled me into a dreamy space and I closed my eyes.

Brett lifted the sheet higher and slipped it over my ankles and up to my calf, stroking the muscle, sliding his index fingers against the back of my leg, moving his hands upward, then stopping at the back of my knee. I moaned in pleasure. *Why didn't I have this done more often?* Using his thumb and fingertips, he pressed the calf muscle and then released it, continuing to knead for several more luxurious minutes.

I flexed my toes. "That feels incredible."

His hands moved upward, working the muscles on my inner and outer thigh. The motion of his hands teased me, and I wished he would move to places he wasn't supposed to.

"Can you go a little further?" I asked quietly.

He stopped, his warm palms resting on my oiled skin. I waited in anticipation to see what he'd do.

Then, slowly, he moved his fingertips higher up my thigh until he just barely grazed the most sensitive part of me.

My tension melted. "Perfect."

In silence, he continued, touching me just enough to make me want more. I felt myself getting wet, and wondered if he noticed.

"Are you good?" he asked in a low whisper.

"Yes." My soft voice cracked. "Yes," I answered again.

"Can I go further?" he asked.

"Is the door locked?"

I lifted my head up and watched him step toward the handle and turn the latch. "It is now."

"Is this a regular part of your service?" I asked, wanting to feel special.

"Not usually." A smile curled into his dimpled cheek as his eyes traveled over the outline of my body. "But I like the way you feel."

I chose to believe him, to give in to the fantasy. I wanted someone young and new, someone with good hands and no ties or complications. Brett's touch felt skilled and attentive. I ached for more.

"Can I keep going?" he asked.

I nodded and smiled into the headrest as I settled back onto the table. The idea of getting carried away was already turning me on.

He placed the heels of his hands into the back of my thigh and applied pressure, sliding in a slow upward motion. I arched my back and spread my legs apart a bit wider. Brett lifted the soft sheet just enough, and asked me in a hungry whisper to turn over. I agreed, slowing turning my exposed body to lie on my back.

He massaged my breasts and then my hips, then pressing his mouth into the exposed flesh of my inner thigh, his lips caressed my skin. Moving upward and inside of me, he teased me with his tongue, tasting me, breathing in my scent. He was warm, and gentle, and extremely detailed.

When he stopped, he asked me to give him a moment. I watched as he removed his socks and shoes, and then his khaki pants and powder blue top. I took in all of him, his body naked, muscular, tan, ideal proportions and to my delight, well groomed. Closing my eyes again and breathing in, I listened to him fumble through a drawer. Foil ripped. He had protection.

He asked me flip back over onto my belly and I complied, thrilled with anticipation over whatever would come next. His knee brushed against my outer thigh as he lifted himself onto the top of the massage table and straddled me in between his knees. Brett massaged my lower back and butt, moving a little lower with every touch. Kneading his thumbs into the tiny crevices of my lower buttox, "Are you sure you're good?"

"Yes." I inhaled as he kissed my back, my shoulders, my neck. He combed his fingers through my hair, nuzzling into my ear with the slightest touch of his tongue.

I wanted to flip over and kiss him full on the lips, but I resisted. He was in charge and I liked it. I had his complete attention. The thought of that alone turned me on.

Brett placed his arms on the table on either side of my back, his strong forearms just barely touching me. As he lifted himself, I felt his legs move to my inner thighs. Brett entered me from behind, gently and then with force as his need for me heightened. His breathing became labored. Gasping, I gripped the edges of the massage table and braced myself for the rhythm of his hips. He lowered himself on one elbow and reached a free hand around my waist and down my pelvis, his fingers rubbing my most sensitive spot as he moved inside of me, bringing me closer to that place.

"You feel so fucking amazing," he whispered.

Just as I was approaching climax, Brett's breathe came faster, his movement more urgent. I could tell he was there when he moaned his release in my ear.

He breathed heavy into my neck and pulled out slow. I rolled over on to my back to face him. Still underneath his warm body, he slipped the condom off and assured me as he looked in my eyes not to worry. "I'm not done with you," he promised with a sexy smile.

He moved a hand to one breast and fondled my nipple as he nibbled the other breast with his mouth. It had been so long since a man had touched my breasts this way, I had almost forgotten how much it turned me on. His touch made me desperate. The way he teased me and made me want him was almost enough to bring me to climax. He made his way down my belly, kissing and licking my skin along his way while his fingers and thumbs continued to pinch and tease my nipple until he reached my inner thigh. Brett bit the delicate insides of my thighs, before fully moving in between my legs. His tongue reached inside me, in then out, licking side to side, up and down, pressing his lips as we explored me. His fingers moved alongside his tongue, as if they knew the territory well. I breathed in and bit my lip hard, aware that any noises could be heard through the thin gap between the door and floor. "Oh my God," I whispered just loud enough for him to hear my need for more. I looked up at the wood beam ceiling and dug my nails into the massage table. With my encouragement, he continued on more feverishly. Moving my hips, I stifled a moan, my entire body shivering.

The room grew smaller, warmer, more intimate than it already was. I wanted him to keep going, but craved the final rush. My mind went blank and all I felt was pleasure. The orgasm came fast and intense. I shuddered in release, my whole body shaking. All the stress had been washed clean in one big wave of overwhelming pleasure. As I sank into the table, I barely registered the tranquil sounds of the rainforest playing in the background. I was completely satisfied.

NATALIE: MONDAY NIGHT
OCTOBER 27

I crawled under the soft comforter of my king sized bed. With my laptop, I signed on to Facebook. I wanted to numb my thoughts, to check out other people's versions of their best lives.

Snuggling deeper into the mint sheets, a message showed that Alik had sent me a friend request. I hit the accept button, and he popped up in my chat.

Hey, Natalie. Thanks for the add.

His quick response was so unexpected it startled me. I sat up straighter in the bed and pulled the bedside lamp closer. *Sure. Didn't think you would be on.*

I'm stalking you.

I bit the inside of my cheek. *How exciting. I'm lying in bed with my hair in a knot and no makeup. Bet you wish you were here, huh?*

Yes. I'm sure you look beautiful.

You know it. A smile pulled across my face.

Send me a picture.

Forget it. I shook my head as if he could see me. Maybe this was how the younger generation talked to each other on Facebook, but I wasn't going to send anyone a picture of myself lying in my bed, especially looking as frumpy as I did.

The chat box showed that he was typing again. *What did you do with your day off?*

I visited my husband in the morning and he remembered the frat house he lived in during college. Pretty awesome.

That is awesome.

Yep. Undoing my bun, I let my hair fall loose around my shoulders. I leaned my head against the headboard, feeling comfortable, wanting to open up more. *Yeah, he said he remembered how the place smelled like vomit and dirty socks and was always littered with empty beer cans. But he didn't have any real reaction to the memory. It didn't trigger any noticeable emotions. Also, it's almost like he's more relaxed with his mother than with me. When the kids or I go over for a visit, it stresses him out more than anything else.*

That's got to be hard on you.

I just wish I knew what he was thinking. He looks at me a lot, but he never says much. It's kind of strange.

Oh yeah, and my five-year-old son was formally diagnosed with a mild form of autism. It's been a super great week. Really fantastic.

Clicking on the overhead fan, I kicked one of my legs out of the blankets to cool down. As much as I needed to vent, I regretted whining to Alik. He was a kid, he didn't want to hear my grown-up problems.

That must have been scary for you to go through alone. I'm so sorry.

It was. I replied, relieved by his response.

What did the therapist say?

She said my son has Asperger's. Well, technically they got rid of the term Asperger's, so I guess Ben has the syndrome formerly known as Asperger's. It's a disorder on the lower end of the autism spectrum.

Alik wrote back before I had time to wonder what he would say. *Ha. I like the way you describe it. My cousin's son also has the syndrome formerly known as Asperger's. What are Ben's symptoms?*

The standard stuff—inability to pick up on social cues, dislike of changes in routine, unusual facial expressions. The therapist said we're lucky. He's high functioning and we caught it at a younger age. I shuddered at the memory of her words. *Finally acknowledging the truth made me want to crush my head against a boulder.*

My cousin had the same reaction. Although I think she wanted to smash her face against the kitchen cupboard.

A laugh slipped out. I bit my knuckle, feeling guilty I wasn't having this conversation with Mark. His memory was coming back in pieces, but he was not in any position to digest this news or help me make sense of it. And honestly, even if Mark were completely fine, I wasn't sure how he would take the diagnosis. In the past, whenever I brought anything up about Ben being different, Mark would shut the conversation down.

You there? Alik typed.

I stared at the laptop screen, realizing I needed to talk about this with someone who was willing to listen. *I'm here. Sorry. I was just thinking.*

About Ben?

Yeah. It's a shocking diagnosis, even if the signs have been there all along. Of course I immediately think, will he be able to find meaningful relationships, go away to college, marry? Hot tears rolled down my cheeks. The salt tracks dried in their wake. *Worst of all, I feel guilt stricken for bringing this sweet soul in to the world to suffer.*

Can I call you?

I hesitated, feeling weak for telling him so much. *I'm having a pity party, don't mind me.*

I want to hear your voice, cheer you up.

How?

I'll tell you a story.

Tell me the story online.

It's about a gorgeous woman who gets her big break in morning news and moves to Los Angeles. She finds the best therapists in the country to help her son and by the time he goes into third grade, he's made lots of friends and is very happy.

Tears wet my face again, only this time with a sense of relief. His story sounded wonderful. *I love it.*

That's not all.

No?

This woman has a hot young boyfriend who worships her.

Sounds like a lucky lady. Too bad it's not real life.
My fingers tapped the keys, waiting for his response.

It could be.

My heart stopped. This was more than flirting.

Natalie?

Yes?

What are you thinking?

I paused, wanting to steer the conversation away from where we were, feeling guilty that I was secretly enjoying it. I directed my thoughts back to Ben. *I'm thinking I don't know how I'm going to handle it all. At any moment I'm going to make the wrong choice and this fragile universe I am barely managing to balance is going to collapse on top of me.*

I can help you. My cousin found a great program through UCLA for her son, and she's been working with him for the last year. He's made some big strides. That kid is so funny and insightful, you would love him. I could find out more. Would you like me to put you two in touch?

Actually, that would be really great.

I wish I could give you a big hug right now, tell you everything is going to be okay. You'll make it through this. You're a great mom.

My body responded without my permission. I didn't want to think about my real life any longer. I wanted to fantasize about Alik holding me in his arms. *Can I ask you a question?*

Go for it. He wrote.

That night I watched you perform with your band and you looked at me before you sang. What were you thinking?

Minutes ticked by on my computer's digital clock. I wondered if he had clicked offline. Then the little dots popped up telling me he was typing.

Truth?

Yes. I wrote back within seconds, my body buzzing with anticipation.

I was thinking... I wouldn't be able to breathe if I couldn't kiss you.

My pulse quickened and my stomach felt warm, like a love drunk teenager. Alik thought he couldn't breathe if he didn't kiss me. Right or wrong, I knew his words would be replaying in my head for a very long time.

Still, I needed to think before I responded. I didn't want to lead him on.

Are you there? He asked after a long pause on my end.

Yes. I said, twisting a lock of hair around my finger.

Can I ask <u>you</u> a question?

Okay.

What were you thinking when I was looking at you that night?

I bit the tip of my index finger and tried to think of a good answer. I couldn't tell him the truth. I couldn't say hey, I wanted to pull you off the stage and take you somewhere dark and quiet. *I was thinking, I hope you sing well so I don't have to lie about your skills.*

Ouch!

Don't worry. You were fantastic. Best singer I've ever heard live.

Gee, thanks.

That's the truth. You were really good.

You looked hot in that tight black dress. I can't get the vision of you out of my mind.

I bit my finger again, thrilled and embarrassed at the same time. *Thanks.*

You're one of those rare women who is truly beautiful inside and out.

I think I have you fooled.

No way. You're one of the good ones.

Kind of like my co-host Dana? It was a childish comment, nudging him to tell me he liked me more than my co-worker. Still, I wanted to know what she meant to him.

She's a nice girl...nothing compared to you. Why

do you ask?

Heard you two were friends, the kind with benefits.

Just a fling. Never anything more.

Is that what you do? Seduce the women of the newsroom one at a time?

You know it. I have a list, Inna's next.

Good luck with that!

Yeah, she'll be easy. I can tell by the way she blows me off and looks right through me when I talk to her. She wants me bad.

She's playing the ultimate game of hard to get.

Exactly... What kind of food do you like best?

The change in conversation threw me. *Um, I like all types of food.*

Any favorites?

Greek.

Meet me for dinner Sunday night? I'll take you to this really great Greek restaurant.

I'm not sure that's a good idea.

Just as friends. It's in Westwood, close to Inna's.

I rubbed my hand against my heart. His invitation felt irresistible. Besides, there was nothing wrong with two friends having dinner.

SAMANTHA: WEDNESDAY MORNING
OCTOBER 28

Brett sent me a text message. *I'd love to see you again. Busy this afternoon?*

I was standing in my mother's kitchen, two days after our encounter at Salon Sol, contemplating a naughty response. Mom walked in wearing an old Halloween themed nightshirt with smiling jack-o-lanterns and faded candy corns. "Who are you texting?"

I shut off the screen on my phone and shoved it into my back pocket. I hadn't told her about Brett's extra special massage. "One of my friends in San Diego. She wants to know when I'm coming home," I lied. "Cameron's been complaining to her. I guess he's realizing how hard it is to take care of three children all on his own."

The old floor creaked as she shifted her weight and rubbed her hands together.

"What's up Mom? I can tell you've got something on your mind."

She pulled out a seat at the tiny table where we ate all our meals when I was growing up. I could still make out the scratch marks from the pictures I'd drawn and stories I had written with pencils pressed too hard against paper.

"Well," Mom responded, "I was thinking, maybe you should go back home. It's a week past when you were supposed to take off."

I pulled out my phone and set it face down on the yellow laminate countertop. "I don't mind staying here a little longer. Your doctor said it could take a while before you start to really get your energy levels back up. You still need me."

Mom folded her arms and shook her head in disagreement. "You've been gone for almost a month now. It's one thing to take a quick break and collect your thoughts. It's another thing to hide away from your problems."

"Are you kidding me?" I pushed the hair off my face. "I came here for *you*, to help *you* recover from your surgery. And then you had that tumor scare."

The wrinkles near her brow line deepened. "It was benign, just as expected. Besides, I'm doing good now. Look at me. I took the extra time off work to be with you, not because I needed more days to rest and recover." She stood up and walked to one of the white painted cupboards while she spoke. "We've gotten pedicures, taken walks. I've done some food shopping on my own. I feel better now than I did before the surgery. Sure, I shouldn't lift heavy boxes or things like that for another week or so, but I have Elena if I need her. I'll manage."

I crossed my arms and watched her pull out the chipped UC Santa Cruz mug I bought for her my first quarter of college. The school mascot, a banana slug, rested between the blue U and C. "You don't want me here?"

"Honey, I love having you here. If you want to pack up my grandchildren and leave your home in California, I would welcome you and the kids with open arms. But Samantha," she set down her coffee cup and looked at me, "you've spent your entire life angry with your father for leaving you when things went wrong between him and me. You don't want to end up repeating his mistakes."

Tears stung my eyes. "Excuse me?"

"I mean it." She ladled a spoonful of instant coffee into her mug. "Don't look for reasons to hide away from your real life. Halloween is in a couple of days and your children need you right now just as much as you needed your father way back when."

I wanted to smack her. It had only been three weeks. How could she accuse me of being anything like the man who abandoned us? I was simply taking a break, collecting my thoughts - helping my mother heal from major surgery.

I stormed off to my room, slamming the flimsy door as hard as I could.

My ankle-boots clomped across the scuffed floors giving weight to my emotions. I climbed the little ladder and flung myself backward onto the top bunk, swiping away a few rogue tears and wishing the world would disappear.

I wasn't anything like my father. Sophia, Savanna, and Gavin were my priority. They always had been. Everyone needed some down time every once in a while. The kids were safe with their father, they knew where I was and that I was coming back soon. It was a Wednesday and I had planned to leave the following Monday. Gavin was happy to go trick-or-treating with his father. My mother was the ultimate drama queen.

Brushing away my tears, I eventually hopped off the top bed, hit the ground hard, and began packing, tossing my clothes over the Christmas present my father had sent me so many years ago.

"Just so you know Mom," I yelled through the closed door, "I'm packing to go home."

When she didn't respond, I pushed the door open and repeated my words a little louder.

"I heard you the first time, Sammi. That's terrific news. Would you like some help?"

"No. And you don't have to be so condescending." I looked under the bed and chest of drawers, scowling at the dust motes, checking to see if I had missed anything before heading to the one bathroom in the house. "I've almost finished anyway. I just need to get my bathroom stuff." I couldn't let go of all that dust under the bunk bed. "When was the last time you vacuumed under the furniture Mom? God knows what's colonizing in all those balls of dust."

"Have you checked with the airport?" she called back from the living room, ignoring my question. "Shouldn't we make sure you can get a flight out before you pack your toiletries?"

She did make a good point. The Rogue Valley International Airport was not exactly a major hub of travel activity. "I guess it does make sense to call first and see what's available," I said, walking back out of the bathroom.

Mom looked up from her book as I sunk onto the opposite end of the couch. "Might be time for some new furniture. This sofa is older than I am."

"Not quite." She rubbed the worn green tapestry. "We got this when you were a year old."

"I think you've gotten your money's worth." I smiled, feeling my anger subside. "You know, you completely overreacted about my being like the man who left us, but I can sort of see why you might think that."

"I just don't want you to have any regrets. It's easy to shut down and avoid taking life head on when it hurts. But your children have to come first. You have to be strong on their account."

I turned my body to face hers, pressing my legs into my chest and wrapping my arms around them. We hadn't really ever discussed how my mom felt when I was growing up. The focus was on me. "How did you do it?"

"Do what?"

"You know, stay strong for me after Dad left."

She folded the page in her book to mark her spot and set it on her lap, turning herself to face me on the couch. "I didn't feel safe letting go. There wasn't anyone else around to take care of us if I fell apart."

That wasn't entirely true, we had Elena. Also, Mom did have her moments of weakness. There were nights, after tucking me into bed, I could hear her thinly veiled sobs on the other side of my closed door. I used to throw the pillow over my ears to block out the sound. In the daylight, however, I would question if I'd heard anything at all. Mom had breakfast set out on the table each morning and my school lunch packed and ready to go. She pulled herself together each day as if all was well.

I stretched out my foot and rubbed my toes against hers. "I'm sorry I gave you a hard time."

"Don't be. I'm glad you have Cameron and me to give you some space to feel sorry for yourself. I just don't want our help to end up hurting you."

"I get it." I pulled in my leg and leaned over to give her a hug. "Thank you, for everything."

A light drizzle of rainfall pinged Mom's roof. Growing up, that familiar tapping, accompanied by a goodnight kiss from my mom, was my favorite bedtime serenade. I had spent so much time resenting my runaway father, I had forgotten to appreciate what I did have.

Mom wrapped her thin arms around me and squeezed me tight. "I love you Sammi, more than all the oceans."

"And I love you, all the way around the world and back again."

I was finally making some progress in the right direction. Now it was time to go home and rescue my own life.

NATALIE: WEDNESDAY NIGHT
OCTOBER 28

For my non-date with Alik, I wore dark blue-jeans and a low cut yellow blouse. Thanks to a particularly bad traffic jam on the 405, I walked inside the tiny Greek restaurant tucked in along Westwood Boulevard a full twenty minutes late.

Light Mediterranean music played, the melodic sound of a Greek lyre set an authentic tone. Alik sat waiting, fiddling with his smart phone. A glass of wine and appetizers were spread out before him at an intimate corner table. He set down his phone when he saw me and stood to say hello. "I'm so glad you made it. I thought you were going to stand me up." He smiled and gave me a firm hug. It felt good to have a man's arms wrapped around me and I hesitated before pulling away.

"I texted you I was running late. Traffic was worse than usual."

Alik had cut his shoulder length brown hair shorter, which made him look less bad boy and more grown up. "I know. You could have been procrastinating though, getting ready to tell me to forget it."

"No." I shook my head, surprised by his intuition.

"No worries. You're worth the wait." He held out the seat for me before sitting himself down. We both smiled at one another in an electric silence.

"I like your new haircut."

"Oh thanks." He ran a hand through his hair. "I was hoping you would."

"I do."

"Good. Hey, I ordered us some wine. Pinot Grigio. It goes great with their Greek spaghetti." He tilted his glass in my direction. "Stinygiasou."

"To your health," I replied clinking my wine against his.

He was right, I had contemplated cancelling at the last moment. But I felt sure now that meeting up with him was the right choice. I liked being here with Alik. "So what have you ordered so far?"

"I got each of us a salad—they're the best by the way—and some spanakopita and stuffed grape leaves."

A small candle flickered in a red glass jar. I inhaled the soft scents of basil and mint drifting from the kitchen.

"Thank you for coming here tonight." He looked at me. "This is one of my favorite restaurants and it means a lot to me to share this place with you."

"Thanks for ordering ahead." I said, placing the red cloth napkin across my lap. "I'm famished."

"Do you know what you'd like for dinner?"

"Will you choose? I'm tired of making decisions." Sitting so close to him like this outside of work was even better than I expected. He ordered the restaurant's special Greek spaghetti along with a plate of moussaka. The waiter seemed pleased with his selections and Alik said I could try them both and eat as much as I wanted of either of the dishes.

"You are so sweet. Is this how you treat all your girlfriends?" I asked, breaking off a flaky piece of spanakopita and taking a small bite.

He leaned forward and put his forearms on the table. "So you're my girlfriend now?" He smiled.

"No." I waved my hand as if the thought were absurd. "I was speaking metaphorically."

"I don't mind calling you my girlfriend." He tilted his head, seeming to wait for my response. I didn't give him one.

"And for the record, I haven't had that many girlfriends. Dana came on to me and we only saw each other a handful of times."

"Is that so?" I teased.

He shook his head and rubbed his hand across his jaw. "She was the anchor and host of the morning show and I was a lowly production assistant fresh out of college." He looked into me with his deep brown eyes. "She came on to me. You can't blame a guy for being curious."

"I guess. How did she hit on you?"

"She actually called me one day and asked me to come over to her place on Wilshire in Santa Monica, to take a look at her computer. It was giving her some trouble."

"And you went?"

"Sure. I'm pretty decent with computers and she said she needed my help."

"Then what happened?" I quirked my eyebrow.

"Are you sure you want to hear this?"

"Yes," I said without hesitation.

"Well, I knew she might have more in mind when she answered the door."

"Why?"

"She was wearing a tiny pink bathrobe that didn't even cover her knees. Then when she sat down at her desk to show me what was wrong with her computer, she said her neck hurt. One of the other girls had told her I was taking massage classes."

"Really?" I asked with wide eyes. "That was bold of her."

"Yeah, she let her robe slide down her shoulders and one thing led to another."

"Wow, talk about being assertive. Guess she knew what she wanted." I could picture the whole scene in my head and it made me feel incredibly territorial. "Did you have a good time?"

"Of course, Dana's a beautiful woman. Still, it was obvious early on it wasn't going to be anything serious. She doesn't have a whole lot of substance."

Alik took a bite from the other half of my spanakopita. "I like my women a little more complicated."

I twisted the silver band on my ring finger. "I wish my life was simpler. I was happy raising my kids, living my boring suburban housewife life. Some of my friends see being a stay-at-home mom as a death trap. I was content."

"Content is good I guess." He sipped his wine.

"It was better than this. Now, I wake up each morning with a hundred pound weight resting on my chest and a gigantic knot in my stomach, worrying how I will make it through another day. Not that it's all bad. I'm grateful for this job and meeting you and Inna, but all of this stress *cannot* be healthy." I stabbed my fork into my salad. "Pretty depressing, huh? Maybe finding a woman who's a little less complicated wouldn't be such a bad thing?"

Alik placed his hand on top of mine, making my heart beat faster. "I like you, exactly the way you are. Just being close to you like this makes me happy."

Eager to put my emotions in check, I pulled my hand away. "Maybe you need a good therapist. It's not normal to be attracted to women with problems. Especially when you have your choice of the Dana's of the world."

He pushed aside his appetizer plate. "I'm attracted to *you*, not your problems. When I said I like complicated women, I meant I find depth and resilience beautiful. You're in a difficult place right now because you built a life that matters. You care about your sick husband and your son, and you are fighting to make their lives the best they can be. I admire that."

A waiter leaving the kitchen lost his balance and dropped a full dinner plate. Porcelain smashed. Stuffed feta chicken and rice pilaf splattered across the floor. I shook my head at Alik. "I don't think having dinner with a man I'd like to take to bed makes me such a great wife or mother."

"You want to seduce me, huh?" he asked with a wicked smile.

I didn't respond, too embarrassed to acknowledge what I had said aloud. He was probably beginning to think I was just like all the other women who threw themselves at him, not so interesting after all.

Alik filled my empty pause. "It's okay to have feelings. I'm actually thrilled to know you think about me that way. But really, I don't expect anything more from you than what you are giving me right now. Don't get me wrong, I want more." He shrugged, making eye contact. "But I don't expect it."

"What if *I* want more?" I asked, feeling a little frantic.

"I'm not going to let you do anything that would

make you uncomfortable. I care about you too much as a person." He took a sip of his wine. "I truly want what is best for you."

It was the perfect answer. Still, it didn't make sense to me. "Why? We barely know each other," I said, trying to figure out his angle. Why was he was so interested in me?

An older couple walked into the restaurant leaning in close to one another, the woman's sun-spotted arm wrapped around the girth of her man. I felt another sharp stab of jealously, missing that level of comfort and closeness in a relationship.

"I know this sounds cliché," Alik said in a lowered voice. "But I knew you the first time I saw you. When I walked up to give you your news scripts on that first day, there was a strong connection between us. You could feel it too, couldn't you?" He reached back out for my hand.

"Yes." I allowed my hand to rest under the weight of his. Our dinner was testing boundaries. I wanted to give in to my feelings. Yet, shame would not ease its grip, reminding me I was wrong to enjoy any of this. Guilt was not an aphrodisiac.

"So what now?" I asked.

"Now, we wait for our dinner."

"And after that?"

"Maybe we order some dessert. One day at a time."

SAMANTHA: FRIDAY MORNING
OCTOBER 31

Cameron waited for me at baggage claim and gave me a strong, masculine hug when I found him. I hugged him back, reveling in his familiar embrace.

"Welcome home Sam," he murmured.

"Why can't we just stay this way Cameron? Why does it have to end?" I asked, feeling a new wave of hurt break loose in my heart.

He rubbed my shoulders and kissed the top of my head. "This is not the end. I adore you. You are the mother of my children. Like it or not, you're stuck with me for good."

"But you're not in love with me," I whined, pulling away from him and crossing my arms across my chest.

"Come on, let's get your luggage." He took my

hand and gave it a comforting squeeze. "We can talk more in the car."

A hot wind hit us when we stepped through the airport doors. My hair whipped in front of my face. "We're having a Santa Ana?" A lot of my friends despised these harsh winds that blew through the mountain passes. Santa Anas were notorious for fueling wild fires, causing sinus headaches, and similar to a full moon, for triggering strange behavior. Personally, I loved them. They were so quintessential Southern California.

"It's nice, huh?" Cameron confirmed.

"Yeah. It was so cold in Oregon. I forgot what real seasons feel like. I'll take warmth and sunshine three hundred and sixty some-odd days of the year over a bitter chill any day."

Cameron smiled, leading me toward his washed and waxed Lexus. The black paint reflected our elongated images. Once we hit the road, he started talking. "We're all set for tonight. All three of the kids have Halloween costumes and both girls made plans with their friends. My mom is staying here until Sunday. She wanted to go with me to take Gavin trick-or-treating. Some of his friends and their parents are meeting up at our place too. You're welcome to join us or stay home and hand out candy. Your choice."

"I guess it's worth hanging out with your mom for an hour or so in order to go with Gavin. In a couple of years, he isn't even going to want to be seen with us, let alone go knocking on our neighbor's doors asking for candy. Does your mom know you're, moving out?"

"I told her everything, she just doesn't believe me."

"What do you mean?"

"My parents both think I'm making up being gay to get out of the marriage. How ridiculous is that?"

"Denial runs deep in your family." I shook my head in disbelief.

"So I spoke with the kids."

"Without me?" I asked, feeling my throat constrict.

"I thought that's what you wanted. Besides, they were asking questions. Sophia and Savanna knew something was up. I spoke with the girls first. We talked last night before they went to sleep."

"What did you say?"

"I told them the truth. I assured them I love them and their mother more than life itself, but I had also been living a lie."

"And?" I twisted in my seat to get a better look at his face.

"I told them I was gay." He ran his hand through his hair. "It's a different time than when I grew up. They know other kids who are out. It wasn't as big a deal to them as I thought it would be."

"So they weren't upset?"

"They weren't happy. Savanna took it a little harder than Sophia. She was most concerned that maybe I only wanted to have children, her specifically, to prove I was straight. It really bothered her.

"I didn't even think about that."

"Me neither, but I let her know it was quite the opposite. One of the reasons I wanted to be straight was so I could have a big family. She seemed to believe me. Then she wanted to know where I was going to live and what was going to happen with you and me.

Sophia was more concerned about whether or not I had a boyfriend already. She asked if I'd been leading a double life."

My brows bumped together in irritation. "That is *exactly* what you were doing."

Cameron ignored my comment, refusing to take the bait for a fight. "Still, they both reacted pretty well. I assured them I wasn't dating anyone else right now. I promised them I would always be a big part of their lives and even if I did eventually meet someone serious, it wouldn't change my love for my children." Cameron squeezed my shoulder.

"I signed a lease on a two bedroom apartment just a couple of minutes from the house. The kids could skateboard or bicycle there it's so close." He flicked on his turn signal and switched to the fast lane. "The complex has an Olympic sized pool, hot tub, a club room and a really nice fitness area. It'll be like having a second hang out spot, only with better amenities."

I shut off the air conditioning and cracked open my window.

Cameron touched a button on his control panel and closed my window. "It's like a hundred degrees outside.

What are you doing?" Heat waves rolled off the road ahead of us, furious swells of inebriated steam.

I shrugged him off and rolled my window back down just enough to let in some air. "And what about Gavin? What did he say?" He was only six years old. Even if he was more of a mama's boy, he had to be upset his father was moving out.

"I talked with him this morning. He didn't say much at first. He cried when I told him I was going to live somewhere else. He said it would hurt mommy's feelings and she wasn't going to like it."

I felt tears form in my eyes. "My poor son. He's always thinking of his mother first."

"He's going to be okay. I didn't tell him the whole story. He doesn't need to know all the specifics at his age. First graders don't need to know about their parents' dating life.

I told him that Mommy and Daddy still love each other and still love him, they just can't live together anymore. I explained we needed to have two houses instead of one. He actually kind of liked that idea. His big concern was that we were still his parents and we would never leave him. Once I assured him we weren't ever going to abandon him he asked me a lot of questions, like what kind of furniture he could have in our shared room. He wants bunk beds like the girls have at Grandma Marla's house. I told him we could certainly work that out."

I rolled my window down further, letting in a rush

of hot wind. "You don't plan on having any random men over around the kids. Because—"

"Don't even go there. You know I wouldn't do that."

"I don't know anything for sure." I felt the heat rise in my chest. "I caught my husband fucking one of his college students. A boy who looked a lot like our son."

"Stop, Samantha. Now."

The strength in Cameron's tone grounded me. Rolling my window back up again, I turned up the air conditioning. "So Gavin and Daddy will share the boy's room and Sophia and Savannah get a girls' room." I gave him a genuine smile. "I like that idea."

Cameron looked over at me. "I do too. It will be a family environment. You have nothing to worry about."

I nodded in relief. Even if we hadn't done it as a team, telling the kids had been taken care of. "Did they say anything to you about why I was taking so long to come home?"

Cameron shook his head. "Nope, you already explained all of that to them on the phone. They know that Grandma Marla needed you there a little longer." He switched lanes as we neared our exit. "I don't know. The girls may have suspected you needed a little more time on your own, but they didn't say anything."

I let out a small sigh of relief.

"You have a good time?" he asked.

I smirked at the memories. "I did actually."

As Cameron pulled off the freeway and turned

west, I admired the view of the Pacific Ocean, its white caps cresting the dark blue waves. With its promise of unrelenting change and enduring consistency, we were almost home.

SAMANTHA: WEDNESDAY AFTERNOON, JANUARY 14

I ran into my neighbor Jason at our community mailbox. He wore the same maroon sweatshirt I had seen him in a million times before. I wondered why he didn't get his bushy brown hair cut and try to look more presentable. Maybe he could find a replacement mom for his two children if he worked a little harder.

"Weren't you wearing that exact sweatshirt the last time I ran into you?" I teased, hoping he might take a hint and go clothes shopping.

"Nice to see you Samantha. You look stunning as always."

I grinned before I could stop myself. He was probably being sarcastic. "Well, I make an effort you know."

Even if he didn't really look like a man who had recently been dumped by his wife, I couldn't help but feel a little sorry for him. Maybe he was just putting on a brave face, the way I did with Cameron.

"How are you? I can't remember the last time I saw you without the little red wagon you are always dragging your kids around in."

"I'm fine. Grace and Andrew are at preschool. I don't have to pick them up for a couple more hours."

"How nice for you, a little down time."

Jason thumbed through his mail. "Not really. Even with a housekeeper coming every other week, I spent most of my morning straightening up the downstairs and doing all the laundry. I was debating between vacuuming next or running out for a few errands."

"Sounds like an exciting day."

"Very." He shrugged. "Feel like coming over for lunch instead? I have some tasty leftovers in the fridge."

I wasn't sure what to say. Jason and I weren't friends. We'd never hung out before. "I'm flattered, but it's only eleven. I'm not that hungry yet."

"That's okay, we'll forget about lunch and I'll make you a cup of tea. Come on, I haven't seen you in a while, and I could use the company. It'll give me an excuse to take it easy before I pick up the kids." He shut his mail box and pulled out the key.

I removed a couple of flyers and some other junk mail while I considered my options. It would be nice to get caught up on all the Nora gossip. I heard she'd been calling Jason from Guam while I was out of town. "All right, but just a quick visit. I have a bunch of things I need to do too before I pick up my kids from school."

Jason lived at the far end of the neighborhood in one of the smaller floor plans. I worried he could turn out to be someone I didn't want to be friends with. After all, there must be something wrong with him if Nora had to leave the country to get away from him. Then I realized it wouldn't be too difficult to avoid him in the future. I could enter the community from the opposite side of the neighborhood and not have to pass by his house. In the evenings, I was usually surrounded by my girlfriends or my children. He'd have a hard time catching me alone if I didn't want him to.

"We're here." Jason smiled, pushing open the front door and giving his yellow lab, Max, a pet on the head. He waited for me to enter first. "After you my lady."

I gave him a sideways glance. "You are too much, you know that?" I stepped inside and looked around, letting Max lick my ankle. To my surprise, his home was tidy and organized. It didn't look like a place where a wife and mother of two had recently abandoned her family. The windows were smudge-free and bright, baskets full of organized toys lined the playroom, and I couldn't find a single stray sock or dog bone on the floor. "Nice place you've got here Jason. I wasn't expecting it to be so….orderly."

"Did you think we were all drowning over here

without Nora? *Help*," he cried out in a mock voice of distress, throwing his hands in the air, "my wife has left me and I'm a frightened man who doesn't know how to take care of anything on my own."

I gave him a half smile. "Well, you never know."

"We are doing just fine. Remember, I was a proud domestic engineer before I chased my wife away." He walked to the back of the house and laid his mail on the kitchen counter. Max circled around and then plopped onto an area rug in the living room to take a nap.

"So it was you who chased the wife away? How did you manage that one?" I asked, pulling out a stool at the bar and taking a seat.

"Excellent question. I think I bored her to death." Jason pulled out two mugs from the cupboard and filled them with steaming water from the instant hot water dispenser on his sink. "What type of tea would you like?"

"Do you have Earl Gray?"

"But of course. I think I'll have that too." He opened another cabinet and searched inside.

"Why do you think you bored her to death? Did she tell you that?"

He turned and set a cup and tea bag in front of me. "Here you go. Would you like some biscotti with that?"

"Sure, thanks." I dipped my tea leaves in my cup. "Sugar too, please."

"Real sugar or the fake stuff?"

"Real."

"My kind of lady." He nodded in approval. "No, my wife didn't tell me she left me because I bored her. Nora felt trapped. She left me with everything, the kids, the house, the cars, the bank account. She calls the kids on the weekends and tells them she loves them. She tells me she loves me too. But she's not coming back. Family life doesn't suit her. Nora's taking over her parents' company out there and she plans to stay. The kids are going to visit her over the summer."

"That's pretty awful."

"I agree." Jason took a seat next to me and took a sip of his drink. "So how are things with you? I heard through the vast Kingston Court grapevine that Cameron moved out last week."

I nodded. "You heard correctly. I too am a bit on the boring side I suppose. My husband didn't run quite so far away though. He's putting down stakes at the Ocean Air Villas down the road. Oh yeah, and he had the courtesy to wait until after the holidays to take off. That was kind of him."

"Why did he leave?" Jason set down his cup and looked into my eyes like he genuinely cared.

It made me nervous. I pulled out my tea bag and spooned in some more sugar. I hadn't told anyone besides my mother why Cameron left. I wasn't ready for all the pathetic looks and mock sympathy, or for people to take pleasure in sharing the news with anyone who would listen. *Samantha Chase lost her husband to a man. Samantha was such a pain in the ass, she turned*

Cameron against women for good. It gave me a knot in my lower back just thinking about it. "We're just taking some time apart."

"I see. Well, if you need a cooking buddy, I'm your man. I signed up for this great service that brings organic meats and vegetables straight to our door each week. There is more food around here than we can eat ourselves, and I'm a terrific chef. You could stop by some evening. I'll cook, you can entertain the kids."

It actually sounded like a nice idea. The past week had been especially lonely at meal time. I missed the adult conversation over the dinner table. "How about tonight?" I asked without even thinking. "I mean, if that isn't too soon."

"Tonight is great. I was thinking of making lamb chops and green beans, with a side of mashed red potatoes and gravy." He stood up and perused his wine rack. "I also have a nice Cabernet Sauvignon for the grownups. The underage folks can drink apple juice or sparkling water."

"Are you sure you're straight?" I asked trying to sound playful. The last thing I needed in my life was another gay man. "That isn't the real reason Nora left is it?"

"No." He shook his head. "I most definitely like women. Although, life might have been a lot less complicated if I batted for the other team."

"Not necessarily." Gay men could be just as frustrating.

He leaned back against the sink and gave the matter some thought. "I guess you're right. When your emotions are involved, things get complicated no matter what, don't they?"

NATALIE: WEDNESDAY AFTERNOON JANUARY 14

Elizabeth came home in the late afternoon with news that sent me reeling.

As I washed the dishes, she told me Mark hit a rough spot in rehab. She took a seat on the couch while I rubbed hot soapy water over our dirty cups and plates.

"Mark said it might be a good idea to transfer him to a facility somewhere near our hometown in Crozet. He thought he might be able to make better progress in a more familiar environment."

"What?" I asked, in confusion. "How is Crozet a more familiar environment? He's been here since college. This is his home."

"Most of his recovered memories are from his childhood."

"So he wants to go to the East Coast?"

"Just until he's back on his feet."

My hands began to shake; anger and fear mixed together in a thick soup of emotions. The way she put it, it didn't seem to concern either one of them that he would be moving across the country away from his wife and children. "Don't you think it would be better if he stayed closer to his kids? How is he going to build a relationship with them if he can't even see them?"

Eight months had passed since his accident. Eight months of either sitting constant vigil by his hospital bed worrying about his wellbeing, or visiting him in rehab at least three days a week, bringing him home-cooked meals, clean clothes, and helping him shave. He had fully regained his ability to read and was making progress with his fine motor skills.

Emotionally, Mark still didn't tell us he loved us or even missed us, nor had his memories of us improved as much as his memories of life before us. He did however, occasionally linger when his hand brushed against mine. I caught him looking at me once or twice when I chatted with a therapist or another patient. Now he wanted to give up and leave? Whatever hope I held on too about him suddenly felt pointless.

***

Jamie agreed to join me on a late night walk after the kids went down. I was still in a state of shock when

I met her in front of her house. She gave me a quick hug before we took off, sneakers tied, jackets zipped all the way up.

"It's cold out tonight." She hugged her curvy size six self and pulled her knit scarf tighter. Long limbed and unfailingly self-assured, the boys in college used to call her Amazon Blonde. The nickname suited her.

"The weather this time of year is crazy. Summer-hot one day and then freezing the next. Kind of like my life." I shoved my hands in my coat pockets.

"Southern California freezing." She pulled the hood of her jacket over her head. "Where are we going?"

"The beach, I need to put my feet in the sand."

"Got it," she agreed, heading toward the lure of salty ocean air. An impartial moon lit the night sky. "So tell me what happened."

I repeated my entire conversation with Elizabeth. "She said it like it was no big deal, but I could tell she was thrilled."

"She's a possessive woman and he's her only son. I'm sure she would love to have him all to herself again."

"Maybe it was her idea to entice him toward her home and he's just going along with it. If I wasn't so hurt, I would have gone and asked him myself. Instead, I just moped around the house all day until the kids got out of school." We approached the boardwalk and stopped to stuff our socks into our shoes. "Let's just

other for ages. He tells me how beautiful and special I am, believes I can have it all with my career and family. He wants to meet my children. He tells me things like he adores all of my idiosyncrasies. The sound of my voice brightens his day and makes his heart beat faster. And the crazy thing is, I believe him. I don't think he's making this stuff up."

"Why is that so hard to believe? Why wouldn't a man feel that way about you?" Jamie asked.

"I don't know. It's just so strange. Besides how young he is, it's like the universe is waving this tailor-made man right in front of me and daring me to take him." I kicked my toes at the water. "Then I get pissed. It's not okay to feel this way about another man when my husband is recovering from a traumatic brain injury, even if he may never be the same again, may never remember me or love me or want to connect with the kids. I wasn't looking for any of this." I leaned over and grabbed a fistful of sand, tossing it in the water. "This wasn't supposed to happen."

Jamie put her hands on her hips and looked at me. "But it did."

"What are you saying?"

"I'm saying this is your life now. You can only make decisions based on *this* reality."

"You think I should let Mark move if he wants to?" I pulled my hair back out of my face.

"Maybe this is the way it's supposed to happen."

"You're scaring me Jamie. Mark is the father of

my children. Lana and Ben need him. We were completely happy and in love before he forgot who we are. I can't just let him go to Virginia while I explore my feelings for someone else. You don't throw away a good marriage when things get tough." I edged out of the water and onto the dry sand, letting my pants fall back over my chilled calves.

Jamie looked at me dead in the eyes. "Your marriage wasn't perfect."

My mouth fell open. "No one's marriage is perfect. You can't spend nearly two decades of your life with another human being and expect it to be endless hot sex and romantic gestures. It doesn't matter who you marry. If you're in it for the long haul, you better be prepared for shit that isn't going to please you."

Mark had become more closed off in his old age. He also loved us completely. He told me I was beautiful each day, helped with Lana's homework, and surprised me with special lunches and dinners.

I stopped walking and looked back at Jamie. "Let's turn around and go home. I'll visit Mark in the morning, tell him he needs to stay. Lana and Ben would be devastated if he picked up and left us when he's so close to coming home."

"Sure."

Jamie was supposed to be the voice of reason, the one to tell me I was wrong to enjoy the attention of another man. She was supposed to tell me Mark and I would make it through this and our relationship would be even stronger in the long run. Why did it bother me so much that she wasn't saying those words? Why did I so desperately need to hear someone tell me to do the right thing?

SAMANTHA: WEDNESDAY EVENING
JANUARY 14

I asked Sophia to knock on the door. My hands were loaded with bags of French bread, Anjou pears, and a homemade kale salad. I heard Max bark and then whimper as someone pushed him across the entryway. Jason's four-year-old daughter, Grace, opened the door with a wide grin. She was dressed in a crinkled yellow Cinderella costume dress, her long shiny black hair combed into a pony tail. "Hewo Miss Samanta. Hi evwryone. Come in."

My daughters returned her greeting.

Max wagged his thick Labrador tail nearly whacking Grace in the face while Gavin raised both his arms, jazz hand style. "Hello Grace. We're here to play and eat dinner."

"Come in den," she said again. She was so tiny and adorable, she reminded me of when Savanna was that age. "My daddy is cooking dinnuh. I hab lots of toys to pway wid."

"Cool." Gavin strutted inside the house like a six-year-old version of a teen heartthrob. His sisters and I followed.

"Hey, come on in," Jason yelled from the kitchen. "I can't leave Andrew while I've got the stove on."

"Isn't that what the baby gate is for?" I asked, giving him a hard time.

"It doesn't always work. I can't trust the rascal. This two-and-a-half-year-old is far too smart for such contraptions."

"Wait until he turns three. Then you'll really be in trouble." I set down my goodies on the bar in the kitchen. "I brought some extras for the meal."

"Thanks. Bring Darby next time too. She can pester Max."

"Maybe," I said wondering how things would go this evening.

"I got a movie for the girls to watch. It looks like a good not too racy chick flick."

Sophia rolled her eyes behind Jason's back.

I shook my head at her. "I'm sure they'll love it. Thank you for thinking of them."

"We brought our iPads," Savanna volunteered. "We'll be fine."

"And their homework," I added. "Savanna still has

math problems to get done. She can work at the dining room table while I watch over the little kids."

Jason, dressed in the same maroon sweatshirt he always wore, turned away from the stove and looked at us for the first time. "Well, if you need any help Savanna, I'm pretty good with numbers. What grades are you girls in now?"

Savanna tucked a piece of her glossy brown hair behind her ear. She couldn't look more like her father and her brother if she tried. "I'm in eighth. Sophia is a sophomore."

"You got all your work done already Sophia?" Jason asked. "I hear they really load you down these days."

"That's for sure. I'm not done, but I'm taking a break. I can finish when we get home." She pulled her phone out of her back pocket and lit up the screen to check the time. "We probably shouldn't stay here too late. I *do* have a lot to get finished."

I forced a smile, knowing she was eager to leave early so she could spend more time chatting with her girlfriends. "We wouldn't want you to miss a minute of your study time, would we Princess?" I oozed sarcasm. "You can walk home as soon as dinner is finished."

She scrunched her nose at me in irritation. I thanked God Savannah was more of a tomboy. Boys were so much easier than girls.

Jason broke into our conversation. "Great, I think you're all really going to like what I'm making. I'm pan frying the lamb chops with rosemary and garlic, and I sautéed the green beans in olive oil and balsamic vinegar.

"It smells delicious," I inhaled. "All right Mr. Andrew." He shot me a gap-toothed grin as I scooped him up and put him on my hip. "We're going to watch Gavin and Grace play Candy Land."

Grace's eyes lit up with pride. "An-dwu is my broduah."

"And what a nice little brother he is Gracie. You're a lucky girl."

When we finished dinner, Sophia said her goodbyes and took off for home, presumably to finish her homework. Savanna watched over the little kids while I helped Jason in the kitchen.

I scrubbed the plates under warm suds and set them carefully on the counter while Jason tossed them every which way into the dishwasher. "Thanks for having us over tonight. It was such a treat to be here."

"So I'm not a bad chef after all?" He shoved another handful of forks into the utensil section. It was a good thing I rinsed them so carefully, otherwise they would never get clean.

"Dinner was good. I liked hanging out with you and your kids. Even Sophia seemed to have fun."

Jason nodded. "Yeah, Sophia told me her boyfriend is a better cook than me, but I noticed she ate everything on her plate. I think she liked it."

I grinned. "Her boyfriend huh? Did she tell you his

name?"

"Adam I think."

"She told me they were just friends. Thanks for the update."

"What can I say? I'm good at extracting important information out of the ladies. They love to confess all of their secrets to me. I could be really useful to you."

"Good to know. I might ask you to spend an entire day with her. You could gather intel and report back to me."

I turned off the faucet and squeezed the steaming water out of his ragged sponge. "You know if you get the sponge wet and cook it in the microwave for three minutes it kills all the germs."

He put a hand on his hip and gave me a half smile. "I did not know that."

"You might want to try it. Anyways, dishes are done. I'll wipe down the counters and then we're outta here. Your little ones probably need a bath and I need to get Gavin and Savanna to bed."

At the end of the evening, Jason walked us all to the door. Dinner was so much nicer than I had expected. On the short walk home, I caught myself mentally picking out potential entrees and side dishes for our next get together.

NATALIE, EARLY APRIL

Months passed and Sunday night dinners at Delphi became our routine. With each non-date my inhibitions relaxed. I found myself touching Alik's hand when he made me laugh, leaning closer when he spoke, even dropping subtle hints that he occupied a space in my favorite dreams. Spending those handful of hours with him became the highlight of my week.

Alik let down his guard as well, revealing more of himself, his hopes and aspirations. He was the oldest son of three siblings and the first family member on his mother's side to be born in the United States. Although she had moved with her parents as a teenager to the U.S. for a better life, she did her best to raise her own children in her traditional culture. They spent each Sunday morning at St. Mary's Apostolic Church, ate

Armenian food for most meals, and conversed with everyone inside their home, besides Alik's dad, in Armenian. His Italian-American father let his mom take the reins.

There were violent turf wars at his public Glendale high school between the two dominate cultures— Armenians and Hispanics—and Alik struggled to walk the line between the two worlds, not wanting to fully take a side.

He shared with me his five year plan to become a full fledged Los Angeles news producer. His band was putting together their first CD and he was hoping that might go somewhere too. I tried not to openly swoon when he said he wanted to settle down in a few years. His live-in grandparents, who were still deeply in love, inspired him and he believed finding your soul mate was life's greatest gift.

Each night we talked on the phone before I went to sleep. I ignored the bright red flags flapping their cutting edges, stinging my face, and continued to flutter into an emotional space I knew was wrong.

Sometime in early April when the days began to stretch into the nights and an unseasonal tear of Santa Ana winds scorched the populated hillsides surrounding Kingston Court, Alik called to say goodnight.

I hid out in my locked bedroom with the cell pressed close to my ear.

"I can't get you off my mind," Alik told me.

"Me either. You have been a constant distraction

today. I was baking birthday cookies for Lana's class this afternoon and forgot to set the timer. Burned the entire batch. Good thing I bought extra ingredients, otherwise I'd have to sic her entire seventh grade class on you."

"I'm not scared."

"You should be," I laughed. "Twelve-year-old girls are a dangerous breed."

"I'll take your word for it."

"You know I'm right." I dimmed the lights and set my alarm clock. Stretching out on my bed underneath the whirring overhead fan, I twisted a lock of hair around my finger. I imagined Alik lying shirtless in his bed.

"Hey, Natalie?"

"Yes?"

"Do you remember the first time we had dinner together and you said you wanted to take me to bed?"

Heat flushed my face. "I remember."

"Did you mean it?" His lowered, uncertain voice wavered with vulnerability.

I tried to laugh the question off as if it were nothing serious. "Oh, I meant it all right. Not going to do it, but I can certainly imagine it."

"Me too." I heard him sigh. "I thought about you all last night, barely slept."

"What were you thinking?" I asked, the whispers of reason telling me not to go there.

"You really want to know?"

"Yes." My words shot out faster than my mind could process the repercussions.

"I thought you wanted us to just be friends. I don't want to make you uncomfortable or do anything to make you think I don't respect your wishes." He breathed another heavy sigh into the phone, making me want to kiss him. "My thoughts are highly inappropriate."

I twisted the wedding band wrapped around my ring finger and toyed with the hamsa on my necklace. If I agreed to this, I would be crossing another invisible line, taking another step toward infidelity.

"Tell me."

"You sure?"

"Yes."

"I woke up this morning to write a song. I was so inspired by you, I needed to express myself, but I ended up writing something else instead."

"What?"

"I was thinking about what I wanted to do to you. It's graphic. You would probably be pissed."

"I want to see it."

"Why? So you'll have an excuse not to talk to me anymore? Forget it. I shouldn't have said anything."

I wanted to go there, even if it was wrong. It had been nearly a year since Mark's accident. Eleven and a half months of stress, fatigue, and anxiety. Alik filled me back up and gave me the desire to face the day. "I really want to read what you wrote. Will you please send it to me?"

"Promise you won't get mad?"

"Promise. I'll call you back afterward." I didn't want to think twice. I was running with my most basic instincts.

"You're sure?"

"Yes." Impatience pushed me over the edge. How bad could it be?

"Okay, you asked for it. I'll email you the first half. Call me when you're finished, let me know if you want more."

I got out of bed and double checked the lock on the door. Then, stalling for time, I walked quietly into the bathroom to brush my teeth. As I crept back under the sheets, I contemplated ignoring his email. I didn't have to read it. I could tell him I changed my mind.

Running my hand over the keyboard, I tried to imagine what Mark would say if he were here right now. What would he think if he knew what I was about to do? Would he disown me, would he understand? Would he even care?

My fingers typed in the password and opened Alik's email. His words pulled me in.

I woke that morning yearning for her. The morning sun reflected off of her flawless, porcelain skin. I wanted to taste all of her, send her to that place..... until I had nothing left.

Running my fingers slowly between the middle of her breasts, I kept sliding them further down her stomach. I could feel her hips arching up as I got close... her breath getting heavier. Her mouth opened and soft moans escaped as I penetrated her with my hand. She wanted me.

She pulled my hand away and turned on to her side as if she was done.... She turned back to me. Her hand moving slowly and firmly up and down me. She didn't need to touch me...I was ready.

Please.... I begged her.... I needed to be inside her. She moved her hips up against me and I pushed myself in. I had all of her, as close as two people could be.. I have to control myself.... I have to last for her..... be good for her."

My blood rushed to all the right places. I closed the computer and waited for the pounding of my pulse to slow. I wished I hadn't asked Alik to send me his story.

I replayed some of his last words in my head, wanting to stop time and make love to him in an alternate universe where it didn't count as cheating. If he appeared here right now, I knew I wouldn't be able to resist.

After taking a few deep breaths to collect myself, I called him back.

"Was it too much?" he asked without even saying hello.

"No. Maybe. I don't know." I toyed with my wedding band in confusion.

"Do you feel disrespected?"

I bit the edge of my thumb. "No."

"Did you like it?" he asked.

"Yes." I pushed back into my pillow. "I kind of feel like crawling through the phone right now."

He laughed. "Awesome. If I could do that to you with a story, imagine what I could do to you in person."

"I'm imagining."

"I'd love to put my hands on you, Natalie, get in between your gorgeous legs. But I want you to know it's not just a physical attraction—I have strong feelings for you. Not a minute goes by where I don't think about you." He stopped talking and I could hear him inhale.

"Alik? You there?"

"I want you more than I have ever wanted anything or anyone in my life."

"Why?"

"I don't know, I can't explain it. It's like I have this hunger for you and I don't just mean sexually, I mean for all of you. I just want to be with you. All the time. Wake up with you. Kiss you every morning before I leave for work. Come home to you every night. I imagine us sharing meals together, scooting next to you at a two person table because I can't stand to not be next to you. I want you to fall asleep on me at night on the couch." He exhaled another deep breath. "Does that scare you? Is it too much?"

I couldn't hold myself back. I wanted more. "Will you send me the rest of your story?"

"It's a happy ending," he teased.

I was too embarrassed to say much of anything.

"Just send it. I'll call you back."

Curling my toes and tapping my fingers impatiently on the keyboard, I waited.

You're arching your back.... spreading your legs...pulling at my waist...pushing me all the way into you..... I can't take my eyes off you.... my senses overwhelmed....

Deep inside you.... caressing your perfect breasts.... I'm losing myself. Your scent.. is all around me..... so turned on.... so intense.... I can't let go. I want to get behind you.... see you on all fours.... kiss down your back to your perfectly shaped bottom. Spread you apart.... taste you..... lick you from bottom to top....even there... own every part of you.... need to hear your labored breathing...

No part of your body will be off limits to me..... I will touch it all.... taste it all. Your scent.... your sweat.... your juices..... on me. You are the only woman I want this way.

I can hear your faint noises now. Perfect body.. legs spread wide. I'm putting it into you this way now....From behind... pushing even deeper into you.... you are reaching back.... squeezing my hand.... it hurts a little.... no.... more.. harder squeezing on my hand.... I can't hold on much longer. I want your sounds.... loud.... I want them all to know I am inside you...I am giving you all that pleasure. Yes.... I am doing that to her. She is mine!

No more.... I can't resist anymore... our bodies

sweating.... meshing.

You're trembling now.. quivering.. My eyes wide open.... I want to watch it happen. I found that spot..... the one that makes you moan. A little faster and more aggressive now. You're almost there.... arching more and more..... your final rush.

Now my turn. I'm going deeper inside you...my hands gripping tight onto your hips.... that last release. You are my dream come true.

I closed shut the computer and fought the enormous smile stretching across my face. Something was wrong with me. I had a husband. It wasn't right to feel this way.

I sent him a text.

Don't tempt me Alik.

So you're thinking about it?

Just thinking.

If you did, I would love you so hard. You would see how a man could truly appreciate your body. It would be the best you ever had. I promise you wouldn't be the same..... it might ruin you.

Such confidence.

I have a big imagination and I am veeeery detailed. It also helps that I'm so incredibly hot for you..... all I want to do is make you "O."

I touched my hand to my neck. My legs felt weak, my hands clenched.

What would you want me to do for you? I asked.

I would want you to completely lose yourself at that

moment.... completely uninhibited.... fingers dug into me...moaning at the pleasure I'm bringing you. When I see your mouth wide open.... belly pulsating.... nipples hard.. massive wet O... then it's about me, that will finish me.

I wanted to grab my car keys and drive straight to Los Angeles. *My God Alik. That would be amazing.*

I slid deeper into the covers. He made it sound so good, it was hard to keep reminding myself it was wrong.

I think I better go now. I need to stop this before I say something I regret.

Like what?

Say good night to me, Alik.

Good night Natalie. Sweet dreams.

Setting the phone on my night table, I tugged the covers over my chest. His words chiseled away at my will power. *If I could do that to you with a story, imagine what I could do to you in person.*

SAMANTHA: MONDAY, APRIL 6

Anxious customers shuffled in the line behind me, checking their smartphones and perusing the cool glass cases of pre-made sandwiches and unappetizing pastries. Baristas yelled out complicated orders. *Tall nonfat latte, no foam, with caramel drizzle. Grande, quad, nonfat, one pump, no whip, mocha.* They all sounded like a bunch of morons.

Three months had passed since my first family style dinner with Jason and life was falling back into a relaxed rhythm. Now I was sitting here waiting for Cameron, armed and ready to take my next big step.

He walked in wearing his designer button-down shirt untucked and dark blue jeans. I waved him over to our corner table and he smiled in recognition. He looked just like the history professor every student wanted to score.

"Samantha," he greeted me with a kiss on the cheek. "It's always so nice to see you in a crowd of faces. It reminds me of how truly gorgeous you are."

I fought to stop myself from making a smart remark. "I got your coffee and added two sugars and cream the way you like it."

"Thanks hon, I appreciate it." He took a seat and set his phone to vibrate before resting it on the table.

"You know, you can lay off the whole charade." I told him. "We're separated. You don't have to pretend anymore."

"Pretend what?"

"The endearments. The 'hon' and 'you look so beautiful.' That stuff."

Cameron rubbed the new goatee on his chin. "I don't know how to tell you this in a way you will believe me."

I leaned forward. "Try me."

"I'm not faking it. I still care about you. When I see you, I still think to myself, that stunning woman married me. She chose *me* for her husband. Being gay doesn't change those things. I never had to fake my affection or admiration for you."

I took a small sip of my coffee before challenging him again, pressing him for the truth. The fear he never truly loved me drove a knife through my bottomless insecurities. "I think you're just so used to saying those things to me, it's become a habit."

"Not true. Imagine if we lived in a world where you were expected to fall in love and have children with someone of the same sex. So you went out and found a beautiful, intelligent, talented woman. We'll call her Debby. You put a ring on Debby's finger, moved in together, had children together because that's the way it worked, and created a family.

Then one day, you needed to live your truth. You let the people you love most know that you are attracted to men—big, sweaty, hairy men. It may seem weird and difficult for them to accept, but it's true.

Now tell me Samantha, would you suddenly not care for the woman you married? Would you still not look at Debby and think, yeah, if I had to be with a woman, I picked a damn good one? Would you not still care about her, miss her, want what is best for her?"

I rubbed my hands together and rearranged our coffees. A woman at the next table sneezed dramatically into her inner elbow while another woman on her cell phone giggled before covering her mouth as she blushed.

"I guess." I leaned back, halfway giving up my argument. "I can't help but feel like it's easier for you to pretend it was all real, than to just admit you used me."

He pinched his lips together in frustration. "Someday you will believe me." He set down his cup and cocked his head to the side. "So what's up? What did you want to talk about?"

I cleared my throat and sat up straight. "I wanted to talk about our plans. I had a great idea about a job for me."

"Excellent. What are you thinking?"

"Well, I was thinking about photography. You know I've been playing around with it for decades now, not doing anything seriously, just making a little pocket money here and there."

"And?"

A group of women walked in the door, letting in a cool spring breeze. I shivered and pulled on my cardigan. "So, I found this incredible little photography studio in old Del Mar. It's really upscale and sweet. The owner wants to run away to Maui and specialize in wedding photography."

Cameron frowned.

"What?"

"You want to take this business over?"

"Why not? I love photography and I'm good at it. I thought your parents might want to help me out with a loan until I get settled. I could send them gorgeous photos of their grandchildren. It's such a respectable job."

"Sam. It's a business, not a window dressing for your new life. You would have to delve into advertising, billing, hiring employees. Photographers work hardest on the weekends and after-hours when families have time off from work and school. The same times your own children would need you most."

He didn't give me enough credit. "You could watch the kids on the weekends. I could pay the current owner a little extra to stick around and teach me the ropes for a month or so."

Cameron wrapped his hands around his paper cup of coffee. "I already do take the kids every other weekend, and half the time you end up at my place hanging out with us because you miss them. You would be miserable. It'd eat up all of your free time and chances are it would take years for you to get to a place where you could even think about repaying the loan. Listen, I have something to tell you. Some really good news."

I drummed my fingers on the table, waiting for him to continue.

"I had another talk with my parents this week. They were finally able to really listen to me."

I beamed at him, despite the hurt I felt at him for not believing I could run a great photographer's studio. "Cameron. That is wonderful. So they believe you now?

He nodded. "I know right? Four months after I've moved out and they're only now settling into the idea." He picked up his napkin and wiped away the ring of coffee under his cup.

"I still can't get over the fact that they didn't believe you when you first told them. Like you would make something like that up."

"You said it yourself, denial runs deep in my

family. Anyway, we had a great talk. They are feeling much better about everything. And, we discussed the house. They said you could stay there until Gavin turns eighteen."

I kept my mouth shut. This was good news, but I had expected as much. They weren't going to kick their grandchildren out of the only home they'd ever known. What I really wanted from them right now was a loan for my new business adventure.

"Sam, that's more than twelve years living rent free in a gorgeous house near the beach. I thought you'd be thrilled."

"I am. Of course I am. It's incredibly generous of them. I also thought they might want to make sure their daughter-in-law had a proper job to care for their grandchildren. It's not like I wouldn't pay them back."

"Think about what you are saying realistically. You would be clawing your way out of the whole thing after day one. You're imagining the glamour of it all, not the reality of working weekends, vacations, evenings away from your children. Taking orders from cranky clients. Not to mention the day to day drudgery of running your own business. You'll have taxes to deal with, paperwork, updates for the website, a blog."

I frowned at him, realizing he might have a point.

"Trust me Sam, I know you. This isn't a good idea."

"I did hear about a job opening for an office manager at my friend's husband's doctor's office. It pays pretty well and the hours are good. Eight to four, Monday through Thursday."

"Where's the office?"

"Carmel Valley, not too far away. It's a nice place too. They specialize in sports medicine. The Padres and a number of other high profile athletes go there."

Cameron took another sip of his coffee. "I bet they pay health insurance too, in case you ever wanted to make our separation official."

"You mean the 'D' word?"

"Someday you may want that." He peered at me over his cup.

I scooted back in my seat. "I guess the Carmel Valley job would be more practical. Regular hours, steady paycheck. It would be a nice environment without a whole lot of stress." I huffed a sigh of resignation and bit the edge of my fingernail. "It's just so dull. 'Hi. I'm Samantha, single mother of three and an office manager.' Just the way I envisioned my life."

Cameron laughed. "It's a job, not who you are. Sam, trust me, this would be a much better job for you, something you could leave behind at the end of each day."

I shook my head at him and smiled. "Fine. As long as you know, you're taking the kids to school in the mornings. And picking them up in the afternoon at least two to three days a week. I don't want them living in aftercare while their mother makes appointments and manages schedules for the doctor gods."

"Deal. Anything else you wanted to talk about?"

"No, you? Any new hookups or guys in your life?" I teased.

"Nothing to speak of."

"Good." I smiled back at him. I wasn't ready for Cameron to have a new significant other. When that happened, he would pull away from me for real.

NATALIE: TUESDAY, APRIL 7

Mark called to ask if I was going to be stopping by for my usual Tuesday morning visit. It was the first time since his accident I felt like I mattered to him. His request also drew a whole lot of guilt right to the surface. I told him I would be there in an hour and was looking forward to seeing him.

When I arrived, he was sitting on his bed scribbling in a journal. A fluted vase sat on top of his bedside table bursting with purple irises and yellow daffodils.

"Those are pretty," I said, gazing at my favorite flowers. "You must have an admirer."

He set down his notebook. "Nurse Ratched smuggled them in for me. I bribed her big time so I could show off for my wife. Do you think she'll like them?"

"Your wife?"

"Yes, my wife. I used to bring her flowers like this on our dates. I thought if I impressed her enough, she might marry me someday."

"You remember that?" I sat next to him on the edge of his twin-sized hospital bed. He scooted toward the wall to make room for me. "I'm in shock," I said, "that you remembered and that you made the effort to get them for me."

He put his hand on my thigh, the most intimate touch between us in nearly a year. "I'm sorry I've been so distant. It seems like every few weeks I have at least one new memory come back to me. Many of them are about you and they only make me miss you more."

I stiffened. "Why is this the first time you've mentioned this to me?"

He sat up straighter and looked at me. "I needed to make sure it was real. Also, it scared me to think about who I was then and see what I've become."

My eyes narrowed. This was everything I had wanted to hear, and yet I couldn't bring myself to smile. "I don't understand. You've barely spoken to me about anything since you got here. Now you're telling me you have memories of us you've been keeping a secret?" Who was this man I was sitting next to? Why would he do this to me?

Mark rested his hand on my arm. "Don't be upset with me. I put my guard up to protect you."

Anger bubbled to the surface. "Hiding your

feelings doesn't protect me." I moved my body further from his, crossing my arms across my chest. "Not too long ago, you considered leaving here and going to your parents to recover. What were you thinking about then?"

He tried to hold on to my arm as I yanked it away. Angry tears burned my eyes.

"I had this wild fantasy that if I went away and transformed myself back into the man I was before the accident, I could surprise you and the kids. If I didn't get better, I would stay there and set you free." He pulled at his left eyebrow, an old nervous habit of his. "You deserve a full husband. Not a man who doesn't know how to tie his own shoes."

"Why are you telling me this now? Why not continue keeping your memories a secret if that was your plan?"

"Because I've been doing so much better. I finally feel like I might be a good husband for you again. I didn't want to put more stress on you until I could be a real man for you."

Reason fought back at my anger. I had to admit, it was hard for me and the kids to see him so emotionally broken and vulnerable. His thinking was so backward, but in a way I understood. "You should have said something, Mark. I wanted to help. Pushing me and the kids away only made us hurt more."

"I didn't realize I was doing such a good job of hiding it. A piece of me wondered if you knew what I was doing and that you wanted to play along, like you needed a way out."

"Are you joking?" I asked, wondering if what he said was at least partly true.

"I'm so sorry." He looked at me with his eyelids low. "My memories come in bursts. I'll be working on my handwriting and suddenly have a vision of your pretty face or of me holding your hand while you're laughing with your friends on our college campus. I can see the sun shining on your long brown hair. Those glimpses of our old life together make my heart ache for you. I can't put all the pieces together. I don't know if I'll ever remember more.

And then I thought you might not want me back if I wasn't exactly who I used to be. I worried you noticed the way I lingered when I looked at you and you were afraid to let me in." Tears filled his green eyes. He looked shaken, road weary. "Natalie, I love you."

My own eyes went weepy. I'd missed the comfort of those words, the warmth of them. "I love you too," I said, trying not to picture Alik's face.

He put his hand on my thigh. "Even before I recognized you, I started to feel a closeness. I could tell by the way your skin made mine tingle when you touched me, the sound of your voice, the comforting feeling I got when you walked in the room. You felt like home to me. I knew you were someone special." He brushed away his tears with a clenched fist. "I wondered what I did right in my life to deserve someone like you. I'm such a mess right now. I've made so many bad choices and I am so sorry."

A warm rush of emotion made my stomach flip, love and fear fighting for a larger piece of my heart. Could we make this work? "Hon, this is a difficult situation and we're all dealing with it the best we can." I ran my finger across his cheek, ashamed of my own indiscretions. "I've felt so disconnected. I truly had no idea you still loved me. Not at all. Whenever I visited, you just looked through me, and you barely spoke. You talked to everyone else. It's like you wished I wasn't here."

"Natalie," he laced his fingers with mine. "I wasn't looking through you, I was trying to be subtle about looking *at* you. I watched you because I wanted to soak you in, absorb some of you. I tried to hide it because I was afraid if you saw how much I needed you, I'd scare you away."

My lips quivered. I tried to control the trembling. If he had told me sooner he could have saved us both a whole lot of confusion and pain. I wouldn't have felt so empty, he wouldn't have had to worry so much, I wouldn't have allowed another man into my heart. Mark spent nearly an entire year pretending not to care about me. Was it my fault I missed the signs? Had I subconsciously wanted to think I was free to explore? I needed to be strong. That's all I knew for sure. "Mark, I'm your wife, for better or worse. We're here to protect one another."

"I've been so messed up. How could you possibly see me as a real husband?"

"What do you mean?"

"I mean, think of me as your equal, feel attracted to me, or anything else either. I'm not the man who swept you off your feet. I've made big strides, but in many ways I'm still an invalid." He waved to his surroundings, the white sterile walls, the exercise ball, the medical equipment. "Look where I'm at. It doesn't exactly scream Superman."

I nudged his shoulder, wanting to lighten the mood. "I heard you tied a perfect loop on your sneakers last week, all on your own."

"It's true," he nodded. "I've mastered the loop. I was waiting until just the right moment to impress you with my newfound skill."

"Babe," I rested my head on his shoulder, "I don't care about how you maneuver a fork or how quickly you learn to speed-walk. You don't need to remember all the details of our past. I just want you to love me and the kids. I want to know that you are happy to see us and that we're important to you. That's all." I kissed the freckle on his earlobe, showing him I still cared, how his physical form made up the smallest piece of how I felt about him. "It's not that bad here and physically you're not that different. Your bones are all healed. You're walking again. I even like your new scar." I traced my finger down the jagged line on his left cheek, forcing myself to feel something close to romantic love.

"It's kind of badass." I shot him a wicked smile to let him know I meant it. "So what else do you remember? What about the kids?"

"I honestly don't remember anything about Lana or Ben. I don't have many memories past our wedding date, just little snapshots from before then, that's all."

The air conditioning whirred on, rattling in the vent. I really did hate this place. I must have made a sour face after Mark's revelation about the kids because he tilted his head closer to me with a look of genuine concern.

"Hey it doesn't really matter, does it? I still love them. They came from us. They are something beautiful we made together." He traced his finger across the inside of my palm, something I remembered him doing when we first started dating. "People adopt children all the time. I don't need to remember their past or our shared history to love them." He looked into my eyes. "If I have to leave here without you and the kids, I don't think I could make it."

He moved in closer to me, his nose touching mine. "I think about you every day." His breath was on my lips. I folded myself into his arms, struggling to push away my confusion. "I've missed you so much," I said, titling my head upward toward his, allowing him in closer. The familiar curves of his soft lips pressed to mine, the taste of his tongue, the scent of him, it felt genuine and familiar, the promising ember of a new beginning. After several minutes, he slowly pulled away and squeezed my hand. "Thank you."

My body exhaled for the first time in months.

On the drive home, with the wind blasting my face through an open window, I made myself a promise to cut off ties with Alik that very night, no matter how hard it would be to say goodbye.

SAMANTHA: TUESDAY, APRIL 7

I threw on a short-sleeved pink dress and silver sandals the moment I got home. Jason and I had dropped our kids off at their respective pre-school and academic schools and we planned to walk our dogs together. I wasn't trying to impress him, I simply wanted to look pulled together and effortless.

"Hey." I smiled as I opened the door for him. "Let me put a leash on Darby and we'll be all set."

He leaned in through the doorframe while Max wagged his yellow tail in excitement. "Are you wearing my favorite perfume?"

"Am I?"

"Yes. I love that scent on you."

"It's called Kai *'the irresistible fragrance of the tropics.'* I wear it all the time."

"I know. It makes me feel like I'm visiting Maui. Thanks for the vacation."

"You're most welcome." I clicked Darby's leash onto her collar, grabbed a cardigan, and locked the front door. "Sorry about missing our walk yesterday. I promised Cameron I would meet him for coffee. We needed to go over a few things." Darby stood on her back legs and twirled like a desperate circus performer. She was lucky she was so cute, otherwise I might have been tempted to ship her off to Cirque Du Soleil.

"Feel like taking a new path?" he asked. "I discovered a trail leading into one of the hills behind Kingston Court."

"Sure. I should have worn tennis shoes."

"Let's go to the beach then. We can check out the trail tomorrow, if you're up for it."

"Sounds great."

Jason and I had fallen into an easy routine since that first family dinner after Cameron moved out. Over the past several months we walked our dogs together most mornings, and then met up in the evening for dinner with our five kids. I enjoyed his company and often found myself daydreaming about what it would be like to develop something more with him. He wasn't my type. He wasn't gorgeous and he dressed like a sloppy college kid. He was almost too nice, a stay-at-home dad who drank tea in the afternoon with his neighbor-lady friend. But he treated my children like family and he made me laugh.

Reaching the boardwalk, the morning air felt surprisingly warm and comforting. The sound of the waves crashing gracefully against the shoreline fed my spirit. Jason walked beside me, slowing his pace to keep in step with mine, holding my cardigan so I didn't have to.

"So, Samantha."

"Yes?" I asked, inhaling the delicious scent of ocean air.

"There's a restaurant in South Park I've been wanting to try. They only serve local foods and every night is something a little different. Plus, I hear they make killer mixed drinks."

I paused to slip off my sandals as we walked along the boardwalk. "We should go then. Maybe on a Saturday so the kids can stay out a little later than on a regular school night."

"Or we could go just the two of us and leave the kids with my babysitter." Max tugged at his leash while Darby barked at a German Sheppard galloping by. "I already gave her a call and she's free to watch our whole crew this Friday."

He quickened his step and looked straight ahead.

I twisted a lock of my hair trying to buy some time to think. His suggestion made me nervous. "Are you asking me on date, Jason?"

"Sure, you could call it that. There's this awesome place by the restaurant. You've probably been there before, Just Desserts? We could go there afterward for cheesecake." He slipped his hand into mine and I felt the tingle of electricity. We had never held hands before, and I was surprised at how good his skin felt pressed into mine. I pulled free of him.

Jason was not the kind of man you had a fling with. He was a good friend, someone I had grown to depend on since Cameron moved out. If our date didn't go well, it would be awkward to move back to where we were now.

He stopped in his tracks and looked at me. "Why did you pull your hand away?"

I felt the heat in my cheeks burn. "Jason, I … I didn't. I just … I like things the way they are." I couldn't remember ever feeling so flustered with a man before.

He touched my cheek. Before I could stop him, he leaned in and kissed me full on the lips.

It was a deep, slow kiss, passionate and intense. His tongue brushed against my top lip and gave me goose bumps. Jason's hands pulled me in closer, one pressed into the small of my back, the other firmly grasping my hip. I kissed him back harder, then pulled away, fighting to gather my composure. "I don't want to lose what we have. I value our friendship more than I can tell you." I rubbed my hands together in nervousness.

"My girls, they already adore you, and so does Gavin. Plus, I love spending time with Grace and Andrew. I would miss them if we stopped hanging out."

I listened to a wave crash upon the shore. "Taking things to the next level, that's serious. We could jeopardize everything. Besides, you don't even know if it's really over with Nora. Cameron and I, we're separated, not divorced."

He reached out for my hand but I held it out of reach. The dogs crossed their leashes over one another's and neither of us bothered to untangle them. "Sophia and Savanna told me about Cameron. I didn't say anything because I figured you would tell me yourself when you were ready. But, I do know. I'm not worried about Cameron trying to swoop in and steal you back. And with Nora and me, that's definitely over. She moved to a different country, started a new life. When she took the kids for two weeks over the holidays she couldn't wait to send them back. Nora's not cut out for family."

"I can't believe my own girls ratted me out. I guess I know whose side they are on," I pouted.

"Don't be mad at your girls, Sam. They like and trust me, they have good taste." He rubbed my right earlobe between his thumb and forefinger.

"I already know how I feel about you, things couldn't stay the same much longer anyway. I'm too attracted to you to pretend we're only friends." He found my hand and grasped it firmly in both of his. "Let's just give this date a try. If it doesn't work out, then I will be able to let it go. We could be just friends again."

I felt a tear slip from my eye. "God, I don't know what's wrong with me. I usually have much better control of my emotions."

"Is that a 'yes' then?"

"This is so incredibly cheesy. I can't believe this is happening." I leaned over to untangle Max and Darby. "One date. Next Friday. No expectations. And just in case you're wondering, I'm only saying yes because you are such a good kisser."

NATALIE: TUESDAY, APRIL 7

Alik met me for dinner at our regular spot. The owner had left the front door open, letting the warm air circulate around the cozy restaurant. Slipping my purse off my shoulder, I hung the strap on my chair.

Alik had comforted me throughout the most difficult challenges of my life and made them bearable. I was certain my feelings for him had been warped by sorrow and confusion. It was time to let him go. He was young and full of potential. He would find someone better suited for him as soon as I set him free.

The moment he walked in the restaurant, my stomach twisted in loops. His sweet smile was meant just for me. It was as if I'd pulled him out of my imagination. The way his fitted black shirt revealed the masculine outline of his lean body, his freshly cut brown hair, the way he knew exactly what to say to cheer me up—how could I say goodbye to him? He would move on and I would spend the rest of my days wondering what could have been. Someone told me once, everyone has *the one that got away*. Alik was destined to be mine.

"Hey you." He leaned over and kissed my cheek. "Why so serious?"

"What are you, a mind reader?" I smiled, trying to shake off my fears.

"No mind reader, just looking at that tight expression on your pretty face. Plus we usually meet here on Sundays, not Tuesday nights. Something's wrong." He sat across from me and called for our waiter to bring him a drink.

I tore the delicate tissue paper from my straw into dozens of tiny pieces, then rolled them all into a tight ball. "Alik?"

He laid his red linen napkin across his lap. "You're scaring me."

"I don't think we should see each other like this anymore. I want you in my life, but we can't go out to dinner anymore or talk to each other late at night before bed. I need to draw a line between the two of us."

"Why? Is this because of what I wrote you?" He looked as if I had given him a speeding ticket for jaywalking.

"No." I felt the weight of his hand on mine. "My husband's doing much better, he's remembering our relationship. We're talking to each other again, like a married couple. I love him and I need to give him my full attention."

Alik took a sip from the red wine the waiter set down for him.

"It's not fair to you either," I continued. "You're young. You shouldn't be wasting your time Facebooking and having dinner on Sunday nights with an old married woman."

His face crumpled with hurt. "You think this is a waste of time?"

"A waste of *your* time. I'm the one getting the most out of this. You would be so much better off pursuing someone with less baggage."

"You don't need to worry about me. I'm right where I want to be."

"Why?" I asked.

"Because I'm happier when I'm with you."

I picked at a slice of bread. "You'll be even happier when you meet someone who can give all of herself to you." The young waiter, a slim guy about Alik's age with his hair pulled into a long ponytail, came to take our order. Alik asked him to give us a minute.

I launched back into my speech. "This relationship isn't good for me either. I have to start putting all of my focus on Mark. I thought if you and I hung out, if I let go of my defenses for a little while and just embraced my attraction to you, that we would realize how little we had in common. I hoped these feelings we have for each other would fizzle out on their own. Yet, for me, it's the exact opposite. Every time I connect with you, I want more."

"It doesn't have to go any further than this," he tried to assure me.

"It's going to end anyway. The network came to me with a full-time job offer. When I hesitated they said they would hire someone else if I turned them down. Get rid of me altogether. The news director told me everyone is replaceable, so I either commit fully or move on."

He tapped his fork against his empty plate. "That's bullshit. They're bluffing."

"I don't think so. Besides, it doesn't matter. My son needs me around more often."

"Don't you still need a job? Mark isn't going to be able to go back to work anytime soon."

"I have a plan. And that's beside the point. I can't go on living these two different lives for much longer, one here and one in San Diego. It's too hard. Ending our dinner dates and our talks is the first step in pulling away from all this." I pursed my lips. "I'm so sorry I dragged you into my problems in the first place. I took advantage of you."

He broke eye contact and lowered his head. "You didn't take advantage of me. I wanted you the first time I saw you. I did everything I could to get your attention."

"I'm so sorry Alik."

He looked back into my eyes. "There's this cool poem I read. The guy tells the woman he loves he would rather spend three days as a butterfly with her rather than live fifty average years."

"Keats."

"You know it?"

"You're not the only one who can memorize words Mr. 'I-sing-in-a-band-and-make-all-the-girls-swoon.'"

"Let's hear it then." He smiled, leaning back in his chair and waiting.

"It's not really a poem. It is a quote from a love letter John Keats wrote to his love, Fanny Brawne."

"I'm impressed already."

"Hush." I tapped my fingers on the table and tried to remember the exact words. "Okay. Here it is. 'I almost wish we were butterflies and liv'd but three summer days. Three such days with you I could fill with more delight than fifty common years could ever contain.'"

His long lashes lowered, sails at half-mast. "I'm really going to miss you."

"Me too. You gave me hope during the most difficult time in my life. I'm so grateful for having known you."

Walking out of the restaurant alone, I slowly exhaled. It was far too easy to picture Alik sometime in the future with kids and a wife. I envied the woman who would get to keep him.

NATALIE: TUESDAY LATE NIGHT
APRIL 7

The dinner conversation with Alik tore at my conscious. I woke several times during the night, tossing and turning in Inna's guest bed, getting up to brush my teeth, go to the bathroom, or check my phone for messages. I worried he wouldn't respect my choice, and then I worried that he would. Knowing I made the right decision didn't diminish my desire to be with him. I told myself I was infatuated with the way this beautiful man treated me. He made me feel special, desirable, important. It wasn't that I was truly in love with him. This was a low point in my life. I was vulnerable. In time my attraction would weaken and my feelings for Mark would strengthen. I just needed to give it time.

Sometime around three am, the cell phone lying beside me buzzed. I had a text message. It was from Alik.

I sent you a message on Facebook.

I rubbed the sleep from my eyes and propped my head up on my pillows, grabbing the laptop from underneath the bed and pushing the buttons to read his message.

Broken sleep yet again. You fill my mind...distract me from rest. I have to tell you some things before we can no longer speak this way.........Natalie.......I love you......I'm in love with you....in the deepest....... purest.....most true way. To ask me to stop showing that I care for you is to ask me not to breathe.....not to live...... I weigh the consequence of losing you completely.....so yes I will try very hard to hold back my feelings... I need you in my life. Not selfishly want.....need. I was built...designed to love you...it's in my genetics. I loved you before I knew you..this is my fate...my destiny....whether it is yours or not. If I bite my tongue and don't display my heartfelt feelings for you, it's because I love you that much, to make the sacrifice to keep you in my life. My love for you will not dissipate...will not change. I will hurt..die a little as I draw back from you. Please know...I will always be here for you..time and distance will not alter my love.

I stared at the body of the note, reading over particular sentences and then re-reading the message in its entirety. Could he really feel this way? Was it possible to fall in love with someone so deeply in a matter of months? I shook my head and read the message again.

This was dangerous. It wouldn't lead anywhere good for anyone involved. Alik needed to find someone who didn't already have a husband and children, someone who could fully appreciate his love. It was up to me to set him straight.

Alik, I read your note. I texted him back. *Pretty intense.*

I rolled over on my back and waited for his response. When I didn't get one right away, I texted him again. *You there?*

Five minutes ticked by. The phone rang.

"You didn't like it?" he asked.

"I did like it. It just worries me that you feel so strongly."

"Great, you think I'm crazy now. It's too late for me to take it back. I can't undo what I said."

"Alik, someone you care about is pulling away from you and your emotions are getting the best of you."

"You don't think my feelings are real?" He sounded desperate.

"I know it feels real to you right now, but I'm also sure it will lessen over time. You're so young, there are so many life experiences ahead of you that will reshape your perspective."

"With all due respect, you are wrong." I could hear

his breath catch. "My grandmother met my granddad when she was thirteen years old. They were married at sixteen and are still very much in love with each other after all these years. I'm twenty-four, plenty old enough to recognize the real thing when I feel it."

"Sometimes when you're in the middle of such powerful emotions, it's difficult to interpret what is real from what is a temporary sense of loss."

"I'm hurt that you're minimalizing my feelings, but it doesn't change anything."

"I'm so sorry, Alik. I don't think our being friends is a good idea. We shouldn't talk to each other outside of work anymore."

"Do you love me?"

Anger choked out my sympathy. He wasn't respecting my wishes. He was acting as if I were free to do whatever I pleased. "I'm not a kid, Alik. I can't breakup with my husband because I like someone else."

"I'm not asking you to *do* anything. I want to know how you feel about me."

"I care about you. I love being with you, talking with you, thinking about you. It doesn't mean I'm in love with you. I think it's more of that initial rush you get when you first fall for someone new. Lust."

"Will you close your eyes for me?"

"Why?"

"I want you to imagine something. Just close your eyes."

I shut my eyes. "Okay, they're closed."

"Are you lying down?"

"Yes. Go."

"Okay, I want you to picture yourself at seventy years old. Really see yourself. Imagine you are sitting on the couch."

Stretching my body out straighter and flatter on the bed, I splayed out my free arm and imagined myself older. I added laugh lines, a droopy jowl, and deep parenthesis around my mouth. The couch was the same as the one I owned now, brown suede, not all together comfortable. I looked a lot like my mom, only with a better hairstyle.

"Now, I want you to picture me sitting next to you," Alik whispered into the phone.

I saw him there right next to me. He held my hand as we watched television. I rested my head on his shoulder and pulled my cozy blanket up higher on my waist.

"Do you see me?" he asked.

"Yes, I see you."

"Sitting there with you? Is it a happy scene?"

"Yes."

"Then you love me."

I opened my eyes. "Explain."

"I dated my high school girlfriend for seven years—the last two years of high school and all throughout college. She wanted to get married. I bought her a ring. But when I closed my eyes, I couldn't see her sitting next to me when I grew older. I could only see her in my present." He inhaled, and I pictured him lying in his own bed in Santa Monica, in some bare, post-college apartment, his body propped up on pillows, his long legs stretched out before him. "When I think about you, I see forever. I see us sitting on that couch together."

"I don't know what to say Alik. That's pretty damn romantic."

"So what's next?"

"Next, we stop talking for a while, let things cool down."

"Are you sure that's what you want? I'll miss you."

"I'll miss you too, I'm sure of that."

"I love you, Natalie."

"I care about you too. I'll see you at work. We'll say hello and that's it. Okay?"

"I'll do whatever you want."

"Thank you." I hung up the phone and closed my eyes, already wanting to hit redial and hear his voice again. I was in far deeper than I had realized.

SAMANTHA: WEDNESDAY, APRIL 8

I was gazing into the full-length bathroom mirror admiring my outfit when the phone rang. I hesitated, not wanting to get caught up in a call when I needed to get going. This was my second week working as an office manager. The first four days had gone exceptionally well and it was important I continued to make a good impression.

I let it go to voicemail.

Inhaling the rich aroma of morning coffee, I turned back to the vanity mirror and ran a brush through my hair and touched up my mascara. Just last week I got carded buying wine at Trader Joe's. I really did make forty-one look good.

The phone rang again.

Pressing the cell to my ear, I listened to Cameron

talk. "Hey Samantha. Yeah, um, if this isn't a good time I can call you back."

"You called twice. It must be important."

"Yes," he cleared his voice. "I probably should have stopped by last night when I was dropping off the kids. Listen, can I meet you for lunch?"

"Sure. Pick me up this afternoon at twelve. I'll meet you in the lobby."

I hung up and turned back to the full length mirror, determined not to let Cameron's drama worry me. My new white cashmere sweater and black pencil skirt looked fantastic, but I wasn't sure about the shoes.

The phone rang again. "Yes?" I asked, assessing my outfit from a new angle.

"Can we change it to 12:30?"

"You're starting to make me paranoid. This better not be bad news."

Cameron chuckled. "I'll see you at 12:30."

I tossed my phone into my purse and switched to a higher heel. They were my power shoes. I had the feeling I might need them.

**

When I stepped into the lobby fifteen minutes behind schedule, I found Cameron waiting for me on one of the black leather couches. We agreed to walk next door to the small Japanese restaurant. It would be crowded, but I figured it was better than wasting time driving somewhere further away.

The petite hostess with a shy smile asked if we'd like to be seated at the sushi bar. Cameron declined, opting for a more intimate table. My lower back tightened. His posture was too stiff, and he kept making comments about the weather and other people's accessories. Had he met someone new? Was he planning on moving back to Northern California? Whatever it was, it wasn't good.

We settled into a table in the center of the dining room. It wasn't exactly private, but at least we were facing each other and not a sushi chef.

Cameron ordered a rainbow roll, two crunchy spicy tuna rolls and fresh albacore sashimi, along with miso soups and edamame. I rubbed my hands on my knees in nervous anticipation. "So what's up?"

He put a straw in his diet cola. "That was abrupt."

"Are you dating someone?"

"Not really. I think I need to get a shirt that says 'I'm gay. Please approach.'"

I picked up my wooden chopsticks and broke them apart.

"Yeah," he continued talking. "I thought it might make me less intimidating."

"So why are we here then?" I asked.

He blew out a large breathe of hot air. "My parents called."

"Here we go. What did they want?"

"They've decided to do some major renovations on

their house."

"Good for them. Your mother could use a project." I smiled at Cameron. His mom was as spoiled as they come. I had my own concerns, like keeping my new job and raising three children while my husband gallivanted around town advertising for hot young lovers.

"I'm glad you see it that way. They want to move into our place down here while it's under construction."

I set down my chopsticks. "But that could take years. Their house is bigger than that plantation home in *Gone With The Wind*. I can't live with your mother for months on end. We'd rip each other's throats out after five days."

He fiddled with his straw, stirring his soda, making the ice clink against the inside of the glass.

"Cameron," I continued, feeling my blood pressure rise. "I'd rather gargle wasps than live with your mother."

"That's why she wants you to move out."

"What? Where would we go? She's seriously contemplating throwing her grandchildren out of the only home they've ever known?"

"They're not throwing you out. They're allowing you to live there until all the kids are grown. They just need the place temporarily. It's their house, and my mom wants to stay there while her own home is out of commission."

"Seriously, they want to move all the way down here while their house is under construction? Doesn't your mother want to keep an eye on everything? Isn't she worried about what could go wrong if she isn't close by?"

The diminutive waitress delivered Cameron's sake along with our edamame and soups before leaving us in silence.

"Mom hired a capable foreman to oversee everything. They've used him in the past for smaller projects. She thought this would be a great chance for her and Dad to spend some time near our kids and relax for a little while."

"What about us? What are the kids and I supposed to do while she's relaxing in my home?"

"You can rent an apartment in my complex. It could be fun."

"Moving all my crap into storage and packing three children, myself, and a hyper-active Jack Russell Terrier into a claustrophobic apartment sounds like fun to you? Great, maybe you should take all the kids *and* the dog, while I live next door. We can visit and chat every once in a while at the community pool. It'll be fabulous." I crossed my arms and tried to keep my head from exploding. "I can't believe your parents' timing. You just moved out. I just started a new job. We are only beginning to adjust to all sorts of huge changes in our lives. Why are they doing this now?"

Cameron leaned back in his seat and put his hands behind his head. "Dad's getting pressure to resign. He got caught putting campaign funds in the wrong hands.

Mom thinks this would be a dignified excuse for him to step down as mayor and for the two of them to get the hell out of Atherton for a while and let things cool down."

I pushed my fingers into my temples and practiced deep breathing. "So this is really happening? My husband leaves me for another man, I have to go back to work after being a stay-at-home mom for the past seventeen years, and now I have to move into a shitty apartment while my in-laws take over my home? Oh, and who is going to pay the rent on this apartment? I don't suppose you're going to foot the bill?"

"Sam, you just got a new job. Of course I'll help you out if you need—"

"Forget it. This is fucking great news Cameron. Thanks for lunch. I really appreciate your thoughtfulness."

I grabbed my purse and pushed through the crowd to the door. Tears stung my eyes and I could feel my nose turning red. Maybe this was God's payback for not giving my mom cancer.

NATALIE: TUESDAY, MAY 5

Mark met me in the parking lot of the rehab center. He wanted to get outside of his regimented environment and show me one his favorite new spots.

Alongside the pink stucco building, a manicured dirt path led into a small nature preserve. "There is a stream back in here. At night you can hear the frogs ribbiting to each other. Now that I'm fully mobile, I like to come out here sometimes to be alone and think."

I stepped on a dry stick and listened to the satisfying sound of it cracking. "It's so peaceful."

"Babe?" Mark pulled me toward him. "Before we go any further, there's something I need to tell you."

My heart quickened with nearly unbearable anxiety and my underarms prickled with heat. He was going to leave me or tell me he had somehow found out about

Alik.

"Hey." He put his hands on my hips. "Don't look so worried. I just wanted to tell you how proud I am of you. My mom's been keeping me up to date on your blossoming career. I can't help but think I've been holding you back all these years from your true calling."

"Oh." I rested my forehead on his chest in relief. "You scared me."

"Sorry. But this is important."

I lifted my head back up to give him my full attention.

"I've been watching your shows. You're a knockout on television, and you are such an outstanding interviewer. Everyone in that newsroom must have fallen in love with you."

I wrung my hands, thinking of the truth in his words. "Thank you. I didn't know you were keeping tabs."

"You know I fully support you with this. You could be the next Katie Couric if you wanted."

"Well," I said, rubbing the thin silver of my hamsa between my fingers. "They did offer me a full-time job. I've been stringing them along for the past month, but I planned to tell them no. I thought it would be too much upheaval to move our family to Los Angeles." I waited for his response, hoping he would attempt to talk me into keeping my job. I loved that newsroom. It would break my heart to leave.

He ran his hand across the brown stubble on his head. "It would be tough. I'd almost rather move back East and live a quieter life, get back to basics. But I want what's best for you, too." He gave me a tight smile, one that told me he was not fully on board with moving to LA. "If you want to go all the way in your career, we'll do it. We will make it happen." He squeezed me tighter. "You are my life. I want whatever makes you happy. Hey," He dropped my hand and reached into his shirt pocket. "I almost forgot. I've got something for you." He pulled out a neatly folded piece of white computer paper. "I've been working on this for weeks now. Letters and the spelling of words are finally coming back to me. I wanted the first meaningful thing I wrote to be for you."

Yet another round of tears welled in my eyes. "Babe, you're writing?"

"Typing anyway. Mom says my handwriting was always terrible."

"Terrible is a bit harsh."

"Good or bad, the doctors say I'm pretty much done with in-house occupational therapy. I should be able to come home in another week or so. Anything else I need to work on, I can come in for regular appointments."

"They told me that too, but it's so much better hearing it from you. It is such incredible news Mark. I'm so happy."

"Me too. This is the end goal I've been dreaming

about since I got here."

I unfolded his note. "Can I read it now?"

He rubbed the top of his head again. "Sure. Go ahead. It's a list of things I remember that I love about you. That list is the culmination of my year in recovery."

I held out the paper as he looked over my shoulder. The words inside were short, but they crushed me to the bone.

Top Ten Reasons I Love You

1. *I learn from you what I cannot learn on my own.*
2. *My identity is intertwined in you from my earliest remembrance of true happiness.*
3. *Our souls are linked; yours spooning mine.*
4. *You want me, even though I don't deserve you.*
5. *Life began when I met you in school. I wouldn't be me without you.*
6. *You have a gorgeous body that I can't keep my hands off of.*
7. *We fight and make up.*
8. *Your lips are so delicious when you're almost there.*
9. *You still feel electric.*
10. *You are "The One."*

Tears slid down my face. My mind, at war. "This is the best list I have ever read. I can't believe you tapped into all these memories and emotions and you were able to write them."

The impulse to toss aside my own desires and focus on my family struck me hard. I felt like a stray cat stuck in the middle of a West Hollywood traffic jam. I didn't know what I should to do, what direction to turn, where I wanted to be most.

"The energy that newsroom puts off is like taking all the best drugs in the world at once. My mind is expanding, and I'm growing stronger as a person.

At the same time, I want to be here for you and our children. And Ben needs extra help. If we really want him to get over his fears and improve his communication with others, he's going to need one of us working with him every day to enforce the new behaviors and strategies he's working on in therapy. The doctors say weekly visits aren't enough to rewire the brain. Someone needs to be with Ben throughout the day teaching him in the moment, and rewarding him when he makes good choices."

"Maybe I could be that person," Mark said. "You know, assuming he even has Asperger's." He pulled a leaf off a low-lying branch and crushed it between his fingers. "He seems fine to me, just a little quirky."

"I know it's a lot to take in at once." I began walking again, needing to move in order to think. "I truly believe Asperger's is the right diagnosis. The more I read, the more all of Ben's off-beat behaviors make sense.

You have to focus on your own recovery. I'm the one who's been taking him to therapy and I'm in the best position to help him. He trusts me. He listens to my advice. Even if I moved us all to LA and didn't have to make that crazy commute anymore, a full-time anchoring position would still get in the way of his treatment. It wouldn't be what's best for our family." My heart sunk at this final realization. Once again, I would have to sacrifice my own wants for my family. Only this time it felt painful, like I was truly leaving something valuable behind.

"Maybe you could find something local and work part-time here in San Diego? My company is holding my position open for me. I could go back as soon as I get out of here."

"That's really sweet of you to say, and I know you're doing so much better, but I don't think you're ready for all of that yet. It's better you take some time to be at home for a while, get to know your children, continue working on your recovery." I stopped in my tracks and looked at him. A child squealed in the distance, most likely visiting a loved one at rehab. This was a place to be thankful for a second chance. "Mark, I know it seems drastic, but even if we stayed here in San Diego and I only worked part-time, it would still be tough for either one of us to give Ben one hundred percent. The news industry energizes my mind, but it also consumes and depletes me. If I'm honest, the stories and interviews I conduct run through my head for days before I can shake them off. It's like I'm constantly going through detox. And those interviews have mostly been mommy focused. A full-time gig would mean pursuing an even wider spectrum of hard hitting topics."

I began walking again, feeling my resolve strengthen. "Ben is still so young. We have an incredible window of opportunity. I don't want to regret spending this time working on a possible career for myself when I could be building a solid future for our son."

"So…" I tugged at a loose thread on my T-shirt. "I've been giving this a lot of thought. Considering everything we just talked about, I think the best option for us may be to sell the house and move to your hometown for a while. The equity in our home would give us a couple of years to focus on you and Ben. It could also be nice for Lana. She's been struggling and living in a smaller town with a whole lot more attention from both her parents could be good for her right now."

This time Mark stopped walking. "What about you? I don't want you to resent us."

"I don't either, and the career is tempting, it really is. But it's not everything. My family comes first. Giving Ben the best shot at a happy life, making sure you fully recover, keeping our family healthy and strong—those are the things that matter most."

Mark pulled me in for a hug and buried his face into my hair. He let out a sigh. "Natalie, I don't know how I could ever live without you."

I wrapped my arms around him, fighting the fear I was sinking back into myself again. *This is the only choice.*

SAMANTHA: SATURDAY, MAY 9

A warm breeze flirted with my green sleeveless maxi dress, the wet sand pushed in between my toes. It was our third official date. Jason had taken me to a seaside Italian grotto, followed by a walk along La Jolla Shores. "Who knew you were such a catch? Dark, cozy restaurants and long walks on the beach. You'd be a sure thing in the singles ads."

"Yeah, I was wondering if I should give them a try."

"No way." I grabbed him around the waist. "I'm keeping you. At least for now."

"You might trade me in?"

"You never know. If you don't make a move soon, I might have to explore my options." I smiled and tossed my blonde hair behind my shoulder. "Goose, take me to bed or lose me forever."

He laughed at my reference to the movie *Top Gun*. "So you're ready for my next move?"

I squeezed him tighter. "I am."

"I've made love to you in my fantasies. Does that count?"

"It's a good start. How was it?"

"It was awesome. I was a total stud. You were okay."

"Hey," I punched him gently on the arm. "I demand a do-over. Besides, we ought to take advantage of my empty house before I have to give it up to my in-laws."

He leaned in and brushed his mouth against mine, slowly sucking my lower lip. I kissed him back, my hands exploring the nape of his neck and the curve of his shoulders.

***

Jason took me back to my place. I asked him to put on some music, to give me a moment before he came upstairs. I wanted to clean myself up and wash the sand off my feet.

Inside my bedroom, I shut the door halfway. Stripping off my ruffled green dress and underthings, I adjusted the dimmer to low light and drew a warm bath.

Over the rush of water filling the tub, I heard him fumble with the stereo downstairs, music poured out of the home's built-in speakers. John Mayer stroked an acoustic guitar before going into an extended solo in *Edge of Desire*.

I slid into the bathtub and listened to Jason's footsteps climb the stairs and enter my room. A light ocean breeze blew outside the open window.

"Nice view," he said to me.

"Thanks," I called to him, looking over my shoulder to watch him walk closer.

"Wow. Is that all for me?"

"It will be when I'm finished with my bath."

He kneeled down next to me and took the bar of soap. Dipping it in the water, he rubbed it into a lather in between his hands. I leaned forward to give him the full expanse of my back.

"You have such a beautiful shape. Your waist is so dainty and feminine," he said rubbing his warm soapy hands down the length of my back and then reaching around to wash my belly and then up to my breasts.

"You're so detailed." I smiled with appreciation.

"It's my pleasure."

I extended my right leg and gave him full access to my calf and foot. He rubbed each one of my legs and feet with great care.

"What would you be doing right now if we hadn't met?" I asked.

"Nothing as good as this. You ready?" he asked holding out a towel for me.

I stood and began to step out of the bath when he

implored me to stop.

"Why," I asked, watching him lean down and flip the bath mat over. "What are you doing?"

"There was sand on it. I didn't want you to get your feet messy again after we just washed you."

I froze, my head swimming as if I had left my own body.

"Did I do something wrong? Are you okay?"

Was he really doing this for me? Did he care enough to notice such a small detail and go out of his way to pamper me? Tears welled in my eyes. "I'm fine." I reached for the towel he held open. "I just can't believe you did that. That's the most thoughtful thing anyone has ever done for me."

"Flip a bathmat over? Are you kidding me Sam?" He helped wrap the towel around my body. "You're too easy, you know that?"

"No, I'm not," I protested, considering whether or not he was right. Is this how a man was supposed to treat a woman before he made love to her? Why had I never expected more?

Jason pulled his brand new polo shirt over his head as I rubbed his belly and chest. At just over six feet tall, his big frame looked better with his clothes off. He removed his jeans and boxer shorts before picking me up and carrying me to the bed. I slid under the sheets and turned my back to him, wanting to luxuriate in his touch.

He pressed his bare chest against my back. "I love

your silhouette," he whispered into my ear. From my ear, his lips traveled down my neck, lingering along the edges of my collar bone. His deliberate attention made me feel delicate, womanly, wanted. No man had taken his time with me before, not like this.

The palm of his slightly calloused hand found its way gently along my rib cage, down into the hollow of my waist, and finally with a firm hold, wrapped my hip bone in his grasp. The deepening of his breath was enough to coax me onward.

I stretched onto my back, allowing him to cup my breast. "What are you doing to me Jason?" I asked. His touch felt so loving. My back arched and I moaned as his tongue traveled down my stomach, into the inner fold of my thigh. Jason used his mouth and hands at the same time, gently applying pressure in just the right spots.

I couldn't take it anymore, I didn't want to wait. Jason started to move back up my stomach kissing me slowly. I rolled us over and put him on his back. He placed both his hands on my hips as I moved on top of him, straddling my legs around his hips. Taking careful hold, I began to guide him inside me.

"Slow down," he murmured. "What's your rush? Let's enjoy this."

I tried to catch my breath. Tried to let him take his time. This was so different from my other sexual experiences with men. I was used to moving things along to make the man feel good, or in the case of

Bobby and me, laying there and pretending to like it.

Jason held me closer, and pulled me down closer to his lips. "Kiss me some more first."

I put my mouth on his and kissed him, allowing the rough stubble of his beard to scratch across my face. Sliding down his chest, my nipples lightly touched the surface of his skin as I went down. My tongue slipped around the head of him and then up and down the most sensitive area, starting and stopping, going slow and then fast. He ran his fingers through my hair, watching me move. I wanted to please him the way he had been pleasing me.

"Can I put you inside me now?" I needed to feel all of him, nothing between us.

He nodded his head in reply. Songs changed, new lyrics...*Slow Dancing in a Burning Room.*

I slid upward along his torso and kissed him once more, a deep passionate kiss, slow and intense. We were connected in the most intimate way. For once, the constant clatter of running dialogue in my head went silent. It was just the two of us and this feeling, nothing else mattering.

I moved him inside me slowly, not giving him full access. He pressed into me, and I raised my hips to stop him. We stayed that way, my hips keeping me just out of reach, kissing and touching each other, letting the ache build. He breathed out and I breathed him in.

Releasing my last reserves of will power, I let go.

Tension and desire. I screamed out and felt him

push harder inside me as I climaxed. Thirsty and spent, I let my body collapse on top of his. He moved below me, my climax sending him over the edge.

Our heat and sweat mingled and cooled. I didn't want to let him go, didn't want time to move forward. Our lovemaking felt so natural, so shared, like we were perfectly in tune with one another. "That was amazing," I said letting out a deep exhale. "If I still smoked, I would definitely need a cigarette right now."

We lay in silence, my head nestled in the crook of his arm. Crickets chirped from the sliver of my open window. "I hope the neighbors didn't hear," I giggled.

"You weren't that loud. Well, except for your scream at the end."

I lightly punched his chest with my fist. "That was all your fault, I hope you know."

"Go ahead, blame it on me."

"I wish you could stay here with me forever," I said without giving it a second thought.

"If you moved in with me, I wouldn't have to leave you at night."

I ran my finger through a curl in his bushy brown hair. Moving in with Jason would be allowing another man to rescue me, to temporarily fill a void. My newfound independence felt good. "I was also thinking …"

"Yes?" he asked.

"I could drop the kids off with their grandparents on Friday nights and come over to your place for midnight play dates."

He scooped me into his bear arms. "My kids are in bed by eight. Why wait so long?"

"What in the world would we do with all those extra hours?" I placed my arm across my forehead in mock confusion as I rolled out of his embrace.

He squeezed me closer. "Let me show you …"

NATALIE: TUESDAY, MAY 12

I steeled myself for Inna's reaction. It was time to tell her my plan.

We sat in our usual places on her comfy couch, getting all caught up on each other's lives. Over the past eight months I had come to think of Inna as a close friend, and while I didn't always agree with her, I respected and valued her honest opinions.

Clearing my throat, I looked down in my mug, nervous about making direct eye contact. "So, I have something to tell you."

Her body language changed. She pulled off her long-sleeved top and tossed her throw blanket to the side. "What is it?"

"I've decided to leave *Good Morning LA*. I'm handing in my letter of resignation in the morning."

"Can't say I'm entirely surprised." Her words came out stiff, but not angry. "I figured there was a fifty-fifty chance you would go."

I forced myself to look up at her, feeling a bit more confident of my decision. "I've been going over and over it in my mind and I think the best thing to do for my family is to sell our house in San Diego and move us to Mark's hometown for a while."

"Isn't that out in the middle of nowhere?"

"Crozet, Virginia. Sort of. It's near the center of the state. They have incredible schools for the kids and it's close to the University of Virginia, so the people are pretty progressive. Plus it's charming—views of the Blue Ridge Mountains, lots of great hiking trails, wineries."

I could hear the saleswoman in my voice. Inna worked in the news industry and knew what I was giving up. If she could understand what I needed to do, then I couldn't be completely insane. I wanted her to believe I was doing the right thing. "I'm not fond of the whole winter thing, but it's doesn't snow all that much and it could be a nice change for a year or so."

Inna cocked her head to the side. "Okay, so what are you going to do for money? Isn't that why you took the job up here in the first place?"

"That's the beauty of moving there. The cost of living is nothing compared to California. If we sold our home, we could live off our savings and Mark's disability checks for at least a couple of years. Also,

I've been talking with the NBC affiliate in Charlottesville, the bigger town just outside of Crozet. They are more than happy to let me anchor the weekend shows so I can pull in a tiny amount of cash and still keep my feet wet."

"You've given this a lot of thought," Inna rubbed her index finger over her bottom lip.

"I know what I'm sacrificing, Inna. There are so many women out there who have worked their butts off for years and will never get a chance like the one I'm about to give away."

"That's a given," she agreed.

I set down my tea. "Here's the thing. I have become so much stronger because of everything that's happened in the past year. Taking on my dream job and doing it well really showed me I'm more than a mother and wife, that my wants and needs are important too. I don't need Mark or any other man to survive. I am taking away something huge from my time on the morning show. None of this was a waste.

But that doesn't mean my family gets pushed to the side. Now that I can make more time for Ben, I want to focus on his Asperger's therapy. Mark isn't capable of helping him the way he needs. And if we move to a place close to Mark's mom and dad, with a slower pace of life, it could be good for all of us. We'd have a built-in babysitter and someone to drive Mark to all his different doctor's appointments while I work with Ben. We could bond again as a family."

Inna lifted her eyebrow. "And living so close to your mother-in-law won't drive you batshit crazy?"

I nodded, acknowledging the truth in her question. "Elizabeth and I don't agree on everything, that's for sure, and I do have resentment toward her. But I finally stood up to her last week while I was driving her to the airport. I can't believe I forgot to tell you, life has been moving way too fast."

"What did you say to her?"

"I told her Mark and I were considering moving to Crozet for a while but only if I made certain things clear.

I said, 'Mark is your son, and I appreciate all of your help, but he's my husband, and if we're going to live nearby and continue to have you help out, then you need to take a step back. This is my family, my children, and my husband. This is our life now and I am in charge.'

I won't allow her to try and tear us apart or discipline Ben when he doesn't behave in a way she deems appropriate. I know what's best for my son and my husband and my daughter, and even if I'm wrong sometimes, those are my mistakes to make.'"

"Did you really say that?"

"Swear on my life, I said those exact words. Best part was, she barely spoke back. My monster-in-law isn't so tough when I stand up for myself. Wish I would have done it a long time ago." I chuckled at my old self. "I just felt so indebted to her and wanted to be respectful of her relationship with her son. Then I realized she wasn't being respectful of me, and I really didn't owe her anything. She wanted to be there for Mark and her grandkids.

Plus I'm still convinced she's responsible for at the very least encouraging Mark to move back East and leave me and the children behind."

"You grew some balls."

"I did, and as long as she knows where I stand and we aren't living in the same house, I think we'll be okay. Besides, I really want to fall back in love with my husband. Living a slower life away from all the excitement and distractions here in Los Angeles, it would give me the best chance to fix that."

"Distractions like Alik?" She looked at me straight on.

"He's definitely one of them."

She held out her fingers and admired her French manicure. "What did Jamie say?"

"Well," I debated answering her question. I wanted to know what Inna really thought and I figured she would probably take the opposite opinion of anything Jamie said. "Jamie doesn't think it's the best idea. She's not a fan of me living in a small town far away from her and so close to Elizabeth."

Inna nodded. "This may surprise you, but I think family should always come first. You're not worrying about your career when you're getting ready to die."

I tilted my head. Would she have said this if Jamie

approved of the move? Then I realized it didn't matter. I had made up my mind. I knew what was best for me and my family. "Exactly." Raising my mug, I resisted the urge to crawl across the couch and hug her. I was going to miss seeing this woman three times a week.

"Thanks for not fighting me on this. The decision didn't come easy. I kept questioning if I was doing the right thing. You know, maybe working part time in San Diego was best. Maybe Ben doesn't need as much help as I think and the kids would be better off living in Southern California. Maybe I could make the LA gig work if Mark's mom stayed on with us for a little while longer, just until I found a way to balance everything. It was such a monumental decision."

Inna shook her head. "Whatever choice you made, you would question it. That's part of being a mom. We live in a constant state of anxiety wondering if we could have done it better."

A wail of sirens passed by outside, racing toward someone else's emergency.

"That's about it, isn't it? We are destined to be tortured no matter what we do. Man, and I thought the sleepless nights and diaper changing would be the hardest part of having a child. Talk about clueless."

"So what about Alik?" she asked.

I shrugged my shoulders, unable to articulate my feelings.

"You're never going to see him after this?"

"That's the plan."

"I think you need to fuck him." She slapped her palm against her closed fist. "Get it out of your system."

It was exactly what I wanted to do. "What if sleeping with him doesn't work? What if it only makes me want him more?"

"Fuck him again."

"Wise words of wisdom." I smiled at her. "Maybe it would be easier to move on if I never go there."

She picked her throw blanket back up and wrapped it around her legs. "No. I can feel the sexual tension between the two of you. It's heavy. My mom has a saying. It sounds better in Russian because it rhymes."

"What is it?" I took a sip of tea.

"*Nelzya ribku syest i na huy seyst.*"

"Which means?"

"You can't sit on a dick and eat your fish at the same time."

"What?" I choked on my tea in surprise.

"I told you it sounded better in Russian."

I put my hand over my mouth, trying to control my laughter. "I don't really see how your mother's delicate proverb applies to my situation. But I'll keep it in mind."

"Think about it. Nobody gets it all, not even you. Take advantage of what you have, while you have it. No looking back and asking *what if*. No regrets."

SAMANTHA: WEDNESDAY MORNING
MAY 27

"She's dying," my mother said, her voice high-pitched, her words, bullet fast.

Jason, Sophia, and Savanna, along with some guys we hired from the side of the convenience store, were helping me carry boxes up the three flights of stairs to my new apartment. I set the awkward moving box on the landing, sweat dripping through my eyebrows and stinging my eyes. "Who's dying? What are you talking about?"

"Elena. She was hit by a man. She was walking to the coffee shop this morning and he hit her."

I motioned to Jason and my girls that I needed to take the call in private. Leaving the box behind, I headed up the final flight of stairs to our new apartment. I imagined some horrible thug robbing Elena at gun point. "What man hit her? Was she mugged?"

"No. This is Klamath Falls, not New York City. He hit her with his car."

I made my way to the bathroom and shut the door.

Mom continued. "He was backing into a parking spot on the street and he didn't see her."

I felt a small surge of relief. "Well, he couldn't have been going that fast if he was backing up. I'm sure she's going to be fine."

"She's not fine," Mom cried. "I'm calling you from the hospital."

I tried to recalibrate and make sense of what she was telling me. "This is ridiculous Mother. You need to calm down and tell me exactly what happened." I squeezed my knee, leaving a dark red handprint. Elena was only five years older than my mother. She couldn't be dying.

I hadn't thanked her for all she did for me. I hadn't shown her how special and important she was.

"The driver was from out of town visiting family. He backed up his rental car without looking and hit Elena head on. She cracked the back of her skull when she struck the pavement. They're trying to stop the bleeding but it doesn't look good."

My neck stiffened. "Mom. Listen to me. My neighbor's husband survived a near fatal car accident. He was in a coma. He had lots of broken bones and a severe brain injury. He had to go into rehab for a full year. But he's fine now. He came home a few weeks ago. They're selling their house and starting a whole new life. Happy ending."

"That's a nice story," Mom said, a hard raspy edge to her voice. "Elena is a sixty-five-year-old woman who was run over by a pickup truck. I have to go. I can't talk anymore. Love you."

She hung up the phone, leaving me stunned and alone on the closed toilet seat.

NATALIE: WEDNESDAY EVENING
MAY 27

Walking into the dim newsroom, I stopped to take it all in. A few stragglers sat typing at their computers, breathing in the stale windowless air. The rest of the desks stood abandoned, littered with scattered paper, pens, and framed photographs. Police scanners bleeped from the assignment desk. I took a deep breath. I wanted to remember this moment. The moment I said goodbye to it all.

Slipping into an empty editing bay, I pulled up the segments of my final stories, pasting together the pieces I liked best. None of this really mattered. Everything was saved digitally on my computer. I could have a professional do the job later.

I was here to see Alik.

The low swoosh of the edit bay door opening lifted me from my thoughts and I pushed the pause button.

"Hey you," Alik said. The warmth of his hand on my shoulder, as he spun my chair around, caught me by surprise.

"Hey." My body hummed with nervous excitement. Alik crossed his arms as if he were relaxed. The tension in his jawline indicated otherwise.

I grinned and looked him up and down, admiring the way he filled out his dark blue jeans and casual T-shirt. "Nice outfit."

"Thanks," he shrugged. "You look beautiful."

I'd worn my sexiest jeans paired with a flowing red crepe blouse. Smiling in the awkward silence, I glanced back at my monitor.

"Nat, can we go somewhere to talk?"

"Do you have a place in mind?" I wanted to be alone with him, but I was afraid of what might happen.

"My friend has a small studio nearby that he rents out for his art gallery. It's empty tonight. We could hang out before you take off."

"All right," I agreed. "I'll wrap up what I'm doing and meet you there in thirty. What's the address?" I still hadn't decided what I wanted. We were going to say goodbye, that much I had settled on, I just didn't know how.

He texted me the details. "Before you take off, check your desk drawer. I left you something."

"What?" I asked.

"It's just a little something, a late birthday present. It was May twenty-second right?"

"You remembered?" I felt like crying I was so touched. Not even my best friend or my husband had remembered this year.

"It's the day you were born, how could I forget? I would have given it to you on your actual birthday but you were avoiding me and I didn't want to hand it to you in front of everybody. Anyway, it's not a big deal, you can open it later when you get home."

"Thank you." I lowered my eyes feeling guilty for skipping out on him the last couple of weeks. Nevertheless, I was happy to think I might have something tangible to remember him by.

As soon as he left I stepped over to my empty desk, opened the top drawer and pulled out a rectangular box wrapped in soft pink paper with a tiny white bow. Tearing off the paper, I discovered a brown and ivory hardcover book. He had given me a reprint of the letters John Keats wrote to Fanny Brawne. A quick scan of the index section showed it contained the prose I had recited to him on our last date at the Greek restaurant on Westwood Boulevard. *I almost wish we were butterflies and liv'd but three summer days ...*

Turning the page, I found a hand-written note that I would have to remove if I wanted to keep his gift. It read: *Neither time, nor lack of contact will diminish my feelings. You will have a part of me forever. ~ Love Always, Alik*

Pressing the book to my chest, my stomach fluttered and my heart ached.

***

The studio was tucked between a grouping of eclectic buildings along Santa Monica Blvd. Turning into the parking lot, my car's headlights swept across Alik waiting by a dim lamppost outside the back door.

He took my hand and led me inside the cement structure. Its walls were covered in beautiful, somewhat disturbing artwork. Large black and white human-interest photos. Ravages of war juxtaposed against impoverished children playing in a still stream while women washed clothes in its dark waters.

Alik motioned me toward a well-worn leather couch placed in the front of the space. I sunk into its oversized seat as he sat beside me.

"So this is it. You're really going to walk away from your life here?" he asked.

My insides began to shake. I nodded, unable to speak.

"This job could make you a huge star. You'd be able to call all your own shots."

"Or they could fire me tomorrow."

"I guess anything is possible." Alik moved into my personal space, the familiar soapy sandalwood scent of his skin soothing my senses. His presence, the very fact that we were alone, made me want to close my eyes and kiss him—something I'd done in my mind hundreds of times. This was my last chance to experience it for real.

That's when he made his move. He pressed his lips against mine before I had a chance to protest. They were as soft and warm as I'd imagined. Heat shot through my body, stoking feelings and desires I couldn't let go.

He traced the nape of my neck with his lips and slid his fingers through my hair. I allowed my own hands to travel up the inside of his shirt, touching the contours of his flat muscular stomach. His pecs flexed in my grasp as his lips explored my cheek, my earlobe, and then the other side of my neck. Common sense struggled against primal desire. "I can't do this," I whispered.

"You're free to go," Alik said, lifting up his arms and removing his T-shirt.

I hesitated in the silence, unsure of my next move. He reached to the edges of my red blouse, lifting it gently over my head. Leaning into me, kissing me, I felt him unclasp my bra before it slid down my arms and fell to the cushion. "You're perfect."

The lowered lights flickered, sending shivers of courage down my spine. I needed to breathe him in, feel all his skin on mine. The sound of his voice, his smell, his taste. I wanted to dwell in them, relish in them, pull those senses over me, feel their warmth. He pushed his bare chest against mine and I abandoned my inhibitions.

My hands ran along the muscles of his firm back.

His lips danced desperately over my collarbone as we breathed heavily into each other. He looked up and I pressed my nose to his. Holding our faces so close to one another felt like the first touch after a lifetime of isolation.

I kissed him again, tears slipping down my cheeks and wetting our lips.

"I'll always be yours," he said.

I couldn't let him go. Every piece of him felt so good. I wanted more. My hands fumbled with his belt buckle, and I moaned a quiet sigh as he pulled away, leaving my body wet with kisses until he reached the rim of my jeans, undoing the button and then the zipper.

If I didn't stop, I would be lost.

Scooting back, I already regretted the space between us. "I'm sorry." I leaned over and collected my abandoned top and bra. "As much as I want this. I can't."

He reached for my waist. "Please, Natalie. If you leave, I will always wonder what it would have been like to make love to you. To be with you. Just once."

My resolve nearly buckled. I told myself it was better this way. We could be flawless in each other's memories. "I will always wonder, too."

"This is the last time I'll see you, isn't it?" His eyes softened in resignation.

"Yes."

"Can you tell me one thing before you go?"

"Maybe." I sat there vulnerable and heartbroken.

"How do you feel about me?"

The soft hum of the city at night filled the quiet. I willed myself to speak, to say something meaningful. "I've shown you how I feel by sitting here right now, by showing up, doesn't that say it all?"

"No, you've barely said anything, done anything. I'm the one who's all the way in."

"In my mind, I've done a lot. This is huge for me, to be here with you. To have kissed you. I've completely stepped over the line." I didn't want to leave without telling him how much I cared for him. I didn't want regrets for words unspoken. Still, the intensity of my feelings scared me. I loved my husband and my family. My husband loved me. The emotions I had right now could never translate into a real life.

"Natalie." He placed his finger under my chin and looked into me. "When I close my eyes, I see you, and I don't want to open them. I love you. I'm in love with you. In the deepest, purest, most true way. I love you so much, if there were a bigger, better word for what I feel, I would use it."

My heart broke open. It was everything I wanted to hear. I imagined his hands touching every inch of my skin, the two of us making every piece of each other feel whole and satisfied. The same desire reflected in his eyes, the last hope that once the words were spoken, I would stay with him.

"Do you want me to fight for you?" He ran a hand through my hair. "I would break down walls for you

Natalie. I would give my soul to you."

His words gutted me. I never wanted anything more in my life than I wanted him in that moment. It had been so long since I had been this intimate with a man, felt sexy, wanted and cherished while in his arms, so long since I'd done something entirely selfish, just for me. Even during the year before Mark's accident when he was healthy and we were working on things, he never made me feel what I was feeling now.

Touching Alik's face, I ran my fingers down his cheek and along his chin. "I love you too, Alik."

He kissed me again, his breath jagged and heated. He pulled back slightly and spoke across my lips, "I'm going to make you feel so good. You will never have this with anyone else besides me."

Giving in to my emotions, I leaned back on the couch as he tugged at my unfastened jeans, slowly pulling them down, placing kisses on every part of my legs he exposed. Once he discarded my pants, I felt him work his way back up my legs, kissing my inner thigh. My stomach fluttered in anticipation. Looking down at the top of his head, I ran my fingers through his hair. He looked up at me with such tenderness in his eyes. I deserved this one night with him, to know what it was like to be made love to by a man who wanted me so completely.

Lowering himself, he gently used his hand to push my thighs further apart. I inhaled as he blew hot air across my flesh and with soft fingers, spread me into his mouth. Alik's tongue brushed across my folds and found my most sensitive spot, sending a jolt of pleasure through me. "What are you doing to me Alik?"

He didn't answer. I could feel my orgasm building as he continued to please me with his mouth. Slowly he inserted a finger deep into me, finding my center, moving it in and out as his tongue continued to do things I didn't think possible. I had never really enjoyed this before, in the past it was something I wanted to rush through. I grabbed tighter to Alik's head holding him in place as I felt my climax building, his tongue and finger making me feel so good. Closing my eyes, I screamed out just as my orgasm took me. "Oh my God Alik. That was unbelievable."

"Was it a good one?" he asked, lifting his head and looking at me with a close-lipped smile, a mixture of love and pride. I reached out and ran my hands over his shoulders, an overwhelming desire to feel him inside of me. "Can we go further?" I asked.

He stood in response and slid off his jeans.

I watched him search his back pocket, removing a tiny foil package before dropping his pants to the floor. Reaching out to him, he slowly backed away, "If you touch me right now, I won't last."

I couldn't help feeling powerful. He was all mine, I owned this man.

Taking the condom, he rolled it on, all the while looking at me as if I were the most beautiful woman he had ever seen.

"Thank you, Alik."

"Thank you. You have no idea how much this means to me, that you would allow me inside of you. I feel so honored." He lowered himself onto me. His brown eyes looked into mine as I wrapped my legs around his waist and felt him push deeper in me.

"I love you so much," he said, kissing me as he moved. His lips brushed across my shoulder, working his way up to the spot behind my ear as he adjusted his body to go deeper. I gasped at the sudden fullness and grabbed his buttocks to pull him closer, wanting, needing more. I came again quickly and lay beneath him in near exhaustion. I felt him shudder and when he finished, I nudged his hot body off of mine, content to lie beside him on the wide couch. As our heartbeats slowed, I looked up at Alik, "You were right. Nothing comes close to what we just shared."

We lay together, side by side, holding one another's hand. I listened to the din of traffic outside, the rev of a motorcycle engine before the low rumbling sound of it trailing off. Making love to Alik made me feel even closer to him, not what I wanted, but I was grateful for the experience. I would never have to wonder if it was real, and this private memory was mine to keep. I stood from the couch to collect my clothes. "I have to get going."

"Will you call me when you get home? I need to make sure you're safe."

"No. This is the last time we can talk Alik."

I walked away, waiting and hoping for some sensation of guilt or shame for what I had done to make it easier to leave him. When it didn't come, when it was just me alone in my car, driving home with a pain so deep I felt sick, I knew there were many forms of love, and this was to be ours. An empty space. I would be okay. I was making the right decision, yet this space would always be his.

SAMANTHA: WEDNESDAY, MAY 27

Elena died. Mom called an hour after we first spoke to give me the news. I didn't have time to fly out there or to hold Elena's hand. I didn't even have time to say thank you or goodbye.

Jason, the girls, and the men who were helping us, moved the rest of the furniture and boxes into the apartment while I hid inside the locked bathroom and cried. I sat on the linoleum floor under ugly, white lights hoping the fan would drown out the sound of my sobs. God was trying to tell me something. I needed to figure out why so many major things were happening at once.

I heard a light rap on the door. "Sam? It's Jason."

Sniffling, I wiped at my eyes with crumpled toilet paper. "Yes?"

"We've got everything moved in. I'm going to take the girls out for dinner before I pick up Gavin and my kids from Cameron's. Is there anything I can get you?"

"No." I said, barely recognizing my own voice.

"You sure?"

"Yes."

"Okay, if you think of something, just call me. I'll keep my cell phone close."

I listened as he hustled Sophia and Savanna out the front door and the three of them thumped down the long flight of concrete stairs. Pushing open the bathroom door, I peeked around the apartment, my eyes adjusting to the dimmer light. It was a disaster. Boxes stacked from floor to my waistline in every room. I considered taking off and losing myself in a long strenuous run along the beach. The walls and clutter of this tiny three bedroom apartment were going smother me.

Instead I stood my ground, convinced there was a message here for me, some sort of sign that would guide me on how to make something good come of all this terrible loss.

Each of the packing boxes was labeled. *Kitchenware, Linens, Savanna's Clothes, Sophia's Clothes, Gavin's Toys.* I looked up and down the stacked towers searching. Why did I bring all this stuff with us? I should have left some of these things in our house. It's not like we were never going back.

I continued searching the boxes. *Mom's Toiletries, Gavin's Clothes, Cleaning Supplies. Books.* Then I saw it. The box I was searching for. *Keepsakes*.

I took my apartment key and dragged it along the packing tape. Ripping it open, I pulled the box flaps out of my way. I found the first thing I was looking for right away, the beautifully wrapped Christmas present my father gave me so many lifetimes ago. I contemplated whether to open it nicely, as if I wanted to save the shimmering red and white paper, or if I should simply rip it open. After having waited three decades, I decided to just go for it.

Slipping off the curled ribbons, I tore at the festive paper. Tape lifted. Strips of red and white shredded. I removed the pretty gold cardboard lid and reached through thick layers of heavy cream tissue paper. Inside rested another smaller gold box. I shook my head in wry amusement, Dad used to make a big deal about hiding the shapes of the presents he bought for Mom and me. He said it added to the suspense because it made it harder to guess what was inside.

Removing the top of the smaller box, I found his gift, a gold heart-shaped locket with the letters SJ engraved in cursive. Sammi Jane, my childhood nickname. With trembling hands I opened the heart. He had fastened a tiny picture inside, one of him and me, a close up of our faces, Dad's dark haired good looks and my crooked and missing teeth. We both smiled wide for the camera.

Mom had a copy of this picture. She had kept it protected in a photo album for years before I got angry one day and ripped it in half. Mom taped it back together and placed it back in her photo album. Right up until the day I moved away from home for good, I refused to look at it.

Why did my dad go through the trouble of putting together such a beautiful gift for a daughter he was planning on walking away from? I closed the locket and stared again at the face of it before turning it over in my hand. There were words on the back:

I will always love you,

Love, Dad

Did he really mean that? Did it hurt him when I never thanked him for his gift or answered his follow-up calls to make sure it arrived? Squeezing the gold heart in my hand until my fingernails dug half moons into my palm, I cried. Why had I been so stubborn for all of these years? Over time, the longer I waited to open his last present to me, the harder it was to confront. Before he left town, my dad made life feel safe and beautiful. Had I opened this gift when he first sent it to me, would things have turned out different? Maybe he thought I rejected him. Maybe he decided I was the one who didn't want a relationship so it was easier for him to forget about me rather than fight for his daughter.

Setting the locket on a nearby box, I took a deep breath and prepared for my next big search. Halfway into the same "keepsakes" box, I saw it, a beat up camel colored leather journal. Elena's sixth grade graduation present to me. Growing up, I turned to this journal when I felt intense joy, depression, anger or loneliness.

I leafed through the collection of my old stories. Some were scrawled on the thick, ragged-edged cotton paper. Other entries were written on elaborate stationary of pinks, pale violets, and soft yellows, tissue paper thin and taped directly into my journal. They contemplated metamorphosis, sorrow, and the difficulties of change. Memories of junior high, cruel neighbors, gossiping girlfriends, and first kisses played in my mind.

I searched the pages until I found the story I submitted to my UC Santa Cruz's writing department. The one that got rejected.

It was titled *Washed Away*, and it recounted the story of Bobby and me. How I adored him, centered my life around him, and how he used and abandoned me, destroying my trust in men.

True, I had changed some names. My tale also included a large family full of impressionable young sisters, a hip mom, and a genuine best friend—all the things I'd wished I really had. That aside, the story was still mine. I owned what Bobby had done to me and turned it into dramatic art. Sadly, the department's committee didn't find my over-the-top suffering as riveting and universal as I'd expected. They rejected me.

From the other side of my apartment wall, I could

hear the laugh track of some sitcom. Looking back at my words from the perspective of time, I could see my autobiographical account had only revealed fragments of my real story. My actual history was much more painful, and had started years earlier, with a different man.

I made a promise to myself. Even if it made me sick, as soon as I got this apartment organized, I was going to sit my ass down and write the truth.

I knew what my message was.

You can run from your fears and your hurts, lock them away and put on a shiny face for your friends and the mirror, but that garbage doesn't go away. It waits for you.

SAMANTHA THEN NATALIE: SUNDAY JUNE 7

After dropping my kids off at the house in Kingston Court, I offered to grab the mail for my in-laws. It was a gorgeous evening, perfect seventy degree weather with a stunning blue and pink sky, and I had some time to kill before Jason got home.

As I unloaded the mailbox, twisting my arm deeper inside the narrow steel box to search for any crumpled letters, I felt someone watching me. I knew before I looked who would be standing there.

"Hey Natalie," I greeted her, pulling my hand a little too quickly from the box. "How are you doing?" My neck and lower back stiffened. I hadn't spoken with her since our argument over Nora all those months ago.

Meeting my eyes, she nodded her head. "Good."

I pushed the sunglasses resting on top of my head back onto my face. It would be easier to talk to her if she couldn't look directly into my eyes.

"So," I switched the mail from my left hand to my right. "How have you been?" The words were already out of my mouth by the time I realized that in my nervousness, I had just asked her the same question twice.

She scrunched her face up at me in what I imagined was confusion. She was probably wondering why I was bothering to talk with her. I hoped she didn't think I was sucking up because she had become some B-list celebrity co-host. It wasn't like she landed Diane Sawyer's job.

Natalie nodded before answering my question. "Good."

"That's great." I smiled "Yeah. I've been doing good too. You know, overall."

She played with the keys in her fingers, not saying anything.

The sun melted into the horizon in a burst of orange. Elena's passing, everything that happened with my mom, the house, and Cameron, it had changed the way I looked at things. For reasons I couldn't fully understand, I felt a need to make amends with this woman who I'd dismissed so often in my past. Natalie had pulled herself up by the bootstraps and used a tragedy to make her life better. I admired her for that.

She searched for the correct key and slid it inside

her mailbox lock. I'd been thinking about her the last few days, hoping to run into her before she left. I figured this might be my last chance. "So, hey, I heard you're moving."

She peered into her mailbox without looking at me. "Yep, our house sold in only a few days. We got lucky."

"Congratulations. I mean, not just on the house but on Mark's recovery of course, and also your big news job. You've been through a lot of changes," I said, fidgeting with the corner of a piece of mail.

She pulled her hand out of her assigned mailbox and really looked at me. "You too. Huh?"

"That's for sure." I smiled, grateful for breaking some of her reserve. "I just got back from a funeral."

"Oh my gosh." Natalie put her hand over her mouth. "Jamie told me you lost someone dear to you. I'm so sorry. It really has been a rough year for us both hasn't it?"

"It's been a roller-coaster. The funeral was for my mom's best friend, Elena. She was a second mom to me." Tears flooded my eyes, yet another wave of unexpected emotion.

"Losing someone you love is never easy." Natalie placed her hand on my arm gently before slowly pulling it away.

"One minute I'm a disaster and then I feel Elena's presence and she comforts me."

"I'm sure she loved you a lot." Natalie left her

mailbox door open with the key hanging out and dropped a letter in the outgoing mail slot. "Hey. I know it's kind of last minute, but would you like to come over for a quick glass of wine? My mother-in-law just left town and Mark is out with the kids, so it's quiet around the house. You could tell me more about Elena."

I shifted my weight and flipped through my in-law's junk mail as if it were important. Something inside me wanted to say yes, though I didn't want to talk about Elena and start blubbering again. "I don't know. You must be busy with the move and everything."

Natalie tugged at the hamsa on her necklace. "Actually, I wouldn't mind taking a little break. I mean, we have most of our things in boxes so the house is a total disaster... but you're welcome to come over if you don't mind the mess."

"Sure, that'd be great." I gave her a genuine smile. "Let me run in this mail and I'll be right over. I can stay for like twenty minutes, then I'll need to get going. Oh yeah, one other thing." I remembered my juicy gossip. "Did you hear about our lovely neighbor, Beth?"

Natalie turned the key in her mailbox to lock it and smiled. "No. Jamie texted me that something happened but she wouldn't tell me what."

"Well I hate to steal her thunder."

"No way. You have to tell me. I hate it when Jamie tortures me by making me wait to find stuff out."

"OK. It's good." I bit my lip in excitement. I couldn't believe it'd been a full twenty-four hours and Natalie still didn't know. It was all anyone in Kingston Court was talking about.

"Great, I'll see you in a few."

***

Samantha knocked on our side door, the door only friends and family used to enter our home. I waved her in while I pulled out some plastic cups and my last bottle of wine. "Take a seat. I hope a half-empty bottle of Merlot and cheap cups are okay. Everything else is packed." I smiled at her as I removed the cork and tossed it in the trash. I wondered what Samantha was thinking right now, why she had gone out of her way to talk to me. I was also dying to hear the gossip.

After setting down our drinks along with some slices of cheddar cheese on paper plates, I joined her at our breakfast table. "Tell me," I demanded.

She inhaled deeply. "Have you ever noticed Beth isn't around during the lunch hour? Any other time of day, you can't circle the block without her buzzing over you. But it's always safe around noon-ish."

I shook my head. "Never noticed."

"Well, as you know, yesterday was a half-day at the school. Beth's daughter Liora was supposed to be on a play date. The other kid got sick so the mom unexpectedly brought Liora straight back from school.

When they knocked on the door and no one answered, Liora grabbed the handle and threw it open."

"So?"

"Insanity. Beth was all done up in some black leather dominatrix getup, black leather corset, cat woman mask, bull-whip and all. The whole deal. Completely over the top. Her husband was on all fours on the ground with a studded dog collar and muzzle over his mouth. Beth was in the middle of spanking him with her whip when she realized she had an audience." Samantha started to giggle.

"That is not true!"

"So true. Oh my God. Marina from next door heard the mom scream and of course she high tailed it over there. Beth turned around and smiled like she'd been caught on candid camera. First she said something about practicing for a play. Then she said it was all her husband's idea and she was just trying to please him. He scurried off around the corner, still on his hands and knees."

"I'm shocked."

"Everyone is." Samantha. "Although I do believe Beth was new to the whole thing, sexual dominator doesn't fit her personality at all. Plus, Marina said Beth was all red-faced and wide-eyed like a startled baby. Not exactly Miss Tough Girl.

"Oh my God."

"It goes to show you never really know what's going on with anyone in their private lives. It's hard for me to even imagine Beth having regular sex. I'm almost proud of her."

"I feel kind of bad. That is so embarrassing."

Samantha giggled. "Don't feel too bad. She's not just boring old awkward Beth anymore. This is something new to put on her resume of life. Kingston Court Dominatrix. Good lord."

"Makes our lives seem tame." I nodded. "Guess she doesn't have the seven strokes rule."

"The what?" Samantha leaned in looking surprised.

"Marina's seven strokes commandment? I thought she told everybody."

"Spill it," Samantha demanded.

"Oh cool. Now I can tell you some fun gossip." I brushed a piece of loose hair off my lip. "After her twins were born, Marina came up with a rule for her husband in the bedroom. Seven strokes and that's it. If he can't take care of himself in that amount of time, that's his problem."

"That's just mean," Samantha giggled. "I love it!"

"I know. Can you imagine? If I were him, I would just use my hand."

"How does she count? Is that seven strokes both ways?" Samantha laughed at loud.

"No, she's very generous. He gets full strokes. But then that's it. She's very serious about it. Once her twins are tucked into bed, she wants to drink her tea and read her book. She doesn't have time to have sex for hours."

"So sad."

"She said he's quite used to it and he doesn't complain. Thank goodness he doesn't buckle under the pressure."

"That's for sure," Samantha said, taking a sip of her wine. "That is so damn funny. I need to let Jason know how lucky he is. I never make him count."

"Seriously," I agreed.

"Thanks for inviting me over."

"And miss out on the Beth news?" I leaned back in my chair, my arms crossed over my chest. "Jamie is going to lose her mind when she finds out she waited too long to share the gossip."

"Poor Jamie," Samantha said.

"We're terrible. Better watch out for lightening to strike or something like that." I stood up and pulled out a box of butter crackers from the bare cupboard. "So how are you? I can't believe we're both leaving Kingston Court after the year we've had. So much has changed."

"I'm good." She took a piece of cheese and nibbled on it with one of the crackers. "I mean losing Elena has been devastating. Also you probably heard about Cameron," she said, searching my eyes for a reaction.

"Yeah," I took a sip my wine. "Nothing stays a secret in this neighborhood for very long. Not even when there's no whips or limited strokes involved."

Samantha traced her finger around the rim of her cup and grinned at my comment. "Well, maybe Cameron's in to S&M too. Who knows?" She shook her head. "Finding out about Cameron kicked my ass."

"I can imagine." I leaned toward the window and adjusted the tilt on the wood blinds. It was getting darker now that the sun had set. "So the whole Cameron thing really did come as a surprise?" I asked before considering this was Samantha I was speaking with. Bonding over gossip didn't make us best friends. She might fire back at such a personal question.

Instead, she relaxed her shoulders and set down her cracker. "Oh, I was surprised all right. I knew something was up, but I was expecting a woman. Not another man...or boy really. When I walked in on them, his lover called me 'ma'am'."

"No." My mouth fell open. "What did you say?"

"I don't even remember. I just wanted to beat him. In a single moment, my whole perception of our marriage turned sideways."

"Crazy how twenty years of your life goes by like it's nothing and then a handful of months changes everything. I don't know about you, but I expected to retire in this house, watch my children grow up here until someday they'd come visit Mark and me with their own kids." My leg spasmed with anxiety and kicked the base of the table.

"You know," Samantha said, "sometimes we tell ourselves the stories we need to hear."

I couldn't help but think about my relationship with Alik. "I guess."

The front doorbell rang and I chose to ignore it.

She stared into my eyes like a distraught lover. "I started writing after Elena's funeral. I'm turning my suffering into art. Someday you'll be reading my best-selling memoir." She nodded her head as if to encourage herself. "Anyway, I like my life now. It feels good to stand on my own. And besides, as far as I know, there's no danger of anyone pulling me into any kinky S&M scandal in my new hood."

"That's a plus," I agreed.

The doorbell rang again. I asked Samantha to give me a second. She hesitated before standing up. "Listen, I've got to get going anyway. Thanks for having me. I really did want to say goodbye before you left. I know I haven't been the best neighbor."

"I'm sorry it took us moving apart to get to this place." I stood up from my chair.

"It happens when it's supposed to. Good luck with everything."

My heart felt lighter. If Samantha and I could get along, anything was possible. "You sure you don't want to finish your wine? It's probably just somebody trying to sell me something."

She edged closer to the side door. "No, I promised Jason I would be there when he gets home. I'll just let myself out." She put out her hand to shake mine goodbye.

I walked over and pulled her in for a quick hug instead. "Thanks for stopping by. I'll keep an eye out on Amazon for your book."

She gave me a toothy, genuine smile, her beauty nearly overwhelming me before she turned to walk away. "See you again sometime."

The person at the door gave up. I snuck a peek through the blinds and saw a window washing salesman walking with his clip board and business cards to the next house. At least some things in this neighborhood would always remain predictable.

ACKNOWLEDGEMENTS

I would like to thank some of the wonderful people who made this book possible: Josh and Alex for giving me mommy perspective, my parents, Joan McAllaster and Daniel Kammier for providing the kind of life that inspires a woman to write, Shelly Tegen for your endless encouragement, support and content edits, Danielle Foerster the sister of my heart, Olga Rosenmayer my muse, Dr. Ariel Marks for taking the time to go over so many technical details, Emergency Nurse Jennifer Ikerd for answering my on-going medical questions, and Caitlyn Toropova for your much needed line edits.

Thank you to my beta readers for your honest and thoughtful feedback: Amy Woo, Chris Tamaska, Chris Youmans, Christa Yelich-Koth, Hilary S. Taylor, Jamie Holder, Janet Jackson, Jennifer Graves, and Mishell

Rudden.

ABOUT THE AUTHOR

Holly Kammier is a former journalist who has worked everywhere from CNN in Washington, D.C. and KCOP-TV in Los Angeles, to the NBC affiliate in small-town Medford, Oregon. A UCLA honors graduate, she is the author of the memoir, *Could Have Been Holly Wood. Kingston Court*, is her debut novel. The California native and mother of two, lives in San Diego, California close to her family and friends. Co-Owner of Acorn Publishing, Holly is available for speaking engagements and content editing.

www.hkammier.com

If you liked this book, please leave a review on
Amazon, Goodreads, etc. and tell your friends.
Word of mouth is an author's lifeblood.
Thank you so much for reading!

Made in the USA
San Bernardino, CA
03 April 2017